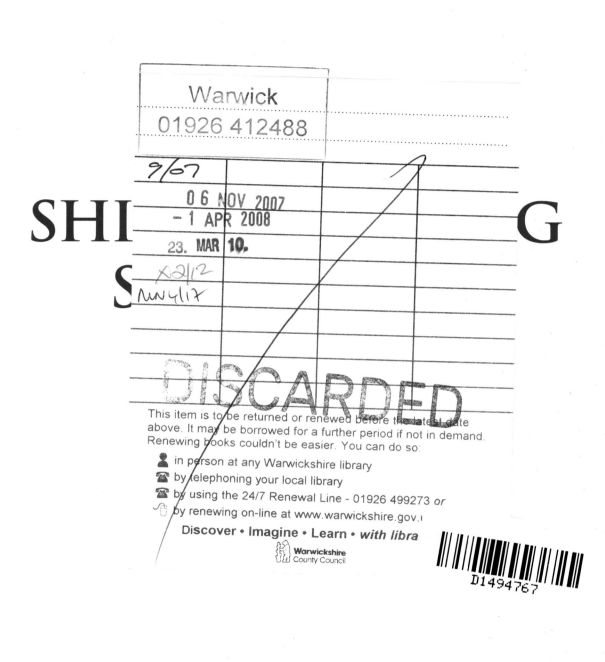

# SHIP MODELLING SOLUTIONS

## BRIAN KING

## SPECIAL INTEREST MODEL BOOKS

Special Interest Model Books Ltd.
P.O.Box 327
Poole
Dorset
BH15 2RG
England



Published by  Special Interest Model Books Ltd. 2007

ISBN  978 185486 247 1


Printed and bound in Great Britain by Biddles Ltd, King's Lynn, Norfolk




www.specialinterestmodelbooks.co.uk

# Contents

| | | |
|---|---|---|
| 1 | Introduction | 10 |
| 2 | Photo Etching for the Clueless | 11 |
| 3 | Toolin' up – Jigs | 16 |
| 4 | Toolin' up – Fixtures | 20 |
| 5 | Press Tooling | 23 |
| 6 | Working to Dimensions? | 26 |
| 7 | The Art of the Masque | 28 |
| 8 | Acquiring a Finish | 32 |
| 9 | The Black Art of Soldering | 36 |
| 10 | Lathe Problems | 40 |
| 11 | Odds and Sods | 44 |
| 12 | Davits | 48 |
| 13 | Aerosol Paint Spraying | 52 |
| 14 | Cowl Ventilators | 55 |
| 15 | Main Armament | 59 |
| 16 | Fittings - 1 | 62 |
| 17 | Developing Compound Angle Shapes | 66 |
| 18 | Shrouds and Ratlines | 70 |
| 19 | Ship's Boats – Open | 74 |
| 20 | Ship's Boats - Closed | 77 |
| 21 | The Bread and Butter Hull – Part 1 | 80 |
| 22 | The Bread and Butter Hull – Part 2 | 84 |
| 23 | Finishing the Hull – Part 1 | 88 |
| 24 | Finishing the Hull – Part 2 | 91 |
| 25 | Rudders | 94 |
| 26 | Propellers | 97 |
| 27 | Seeking Information? | 100 |
| 28 | Anchors – Part 1 | 103 |
| 29 | Anchors – part 2 | 108 |

| 30 | Problems, Problems! | 113 |
|----|---------------------|-----|
| 31 | Decking | 116 |
| 32 | Gun Barrels | 119 |
| 33 | Computers and Modelling – Part 1 | 122 |
| 34 | Computers and Modelling – Part 2 | 126 |
| 35 | Life Saving Gear | 130 |
| 36 | Portholes | 136 |
| 37 | Photographing your Models | 140 |
| 38 | Fittings - 2 | 144 |
| 39 | Making Plastic Castings | 150 |
| 40 | Lines and Sections | 155 |
| 41 | Idea Development | 159 |
| 42 | Simulation | 163 |
| 43 | Ladders | 167 |
| 44 | Bending and Folding | 173 |

# Acknowledgements

I wrote the book but that, as always, is only the start of the process of bringing it to life. I owe a big thank you to John Cundell, Editor of Model Boats magazine where these pieces were first printed. My contract with Encanta allows me to retain copyright after the first publication in Model Boats so I suggested reprinting the Columns as a book, which was accepted by Special Interest Model Books. As usual my right arm person, Azien Watkin, did all the "leg" work including reconstruction of the first 20 columns, which got destroyed by an errant computer. Thanks must go to my friend Roger Antrobus for allowing the use his picture of me. Thanks also to Bill Burkinshaw for his services on this book. If I have missed anybody please forgive me. We happy band all hope you enjoy it.

# Preface

In this age of specialisation, when people in all walks of life concentrate on learning more and more about less and less until they know everything about nothing, the author of this book stands out as a genuine modern polymath.

His modelling career began some years before he won an apprenticeship in the drawing office at Lagonda Motors under the late W. O. Bentley and he has spent all of his working life as a professional engineer. Nevertheless, Brian has a much broader knowledge of English literature than most and is a music enthusiast who takes delight in accurately putting a name to classical performers when listening to the radio. In addition he has enjoyed success as a potter, sculptor and water-colourist, as well as being a keen gardener, an astute investor and more than competent with needle and thread!

Brian is known to most, however, through the outstanding ship models which have won him many national and international awards and in recent years he has begun to pass on his techniques and knowledge by writing books and magazine articles.

All modellers have to analyse and solve challenges but where Brian differs from most of us is that his instinct is to document his solutions rather than hoping he might remember them in the future and these jottings are the basis for this book.

Few of us nowadays have the space to acquire the renaissance polymath's extensive library and collections of specimens from nature but for the ship modeller seeking hints and tips on all manner of procedures from the mundane to the esoteric the viable alternative to a vast collection of magazines is the concentrated wisdom of this book. Therein the simplest of tasks may be seen in a new light and the more complicated are reduced to a logical series of operations understandable by all.

*David Watkin*

# 1. Introduction

This book consists of the one page "Columns" written for the monthly magazine "Model Boats" between spring 2003 and spring 2007. Mostly they were on subjects I chose although some were in answer to enquiries I received. One case in point was a request to develop the shape of the bridge of a Type 22, an ideal subject not only for its direct result but as a teaching aid on the preliminaries of drawing development.

These pieces are a kind of lecture and my experience as a Technical College lecturer has taught me to always keep a sense of humour to avoid boring your class to sleep. I remember once having to teach maths to a motor vehicle class on the first session Friday afternoon, all present except me having consumed a liquid lunch. I eventually decided such a task was beyond all human endeavour and if I managed to keep half of them interested for half the lesson this was all that could be expected of a mere mortal man.

Teaching, whether it be verbally or written down requires interest and the absence of boredom. A little experience allows you to see wandering attention, the glazing of the eyes, etc, which is where you slip in the odd joke, change the speed or change the activity. This is why you will find, I hope, the odd spot of humour in my writing; it is the sugar on the pill! How much sinks in you know not. The editor says the only time you hear anything is when they don't like it (like the Northern drinking clubs – otherwise they let you live).

I have made no attempt to sort them in any order, they are laid down more or less as written and first published with perhaps a word or so changed here and there where, on a read through, I have thought of a more suitable word. Nearly all the illustrations whether photos or drawings have been abstracted from my own model work and illustrate my own philosophy of model making. The models illustrated have been built over the last 30 years and of course show my interests. I suppose my main one is ships of the late Victorian era both in British and other countries' fleets. We had by that time, more or less sorted out the main problems and got rid of a few stupid ideas such as ramming. Fitting great big cast-steel rams on the bows of battleships proved more dangerous to your own side than to the enemy who wasn't likely to stick around while you got near enough to "stick it up 'em" anyway. Steel as the main construction material replaced wrought iron, which was difficult to make anyway, whereas steel, thanks to Bessemer and his converter and Siemens with his open-hearth furnace was much easier and cheaper to make. It has however the disadvantage of rusting more readily compared with wrought and cast iron,

The strange designs of the earlier Victorian period had disappeared such as that seen in the HMS Captain which capsized and sank in a heavy storm taking most of the crew and its designer to their deaths.

As a modeller the availability of plans is a must and photography will supply extra detail if required. Photos always have the advantage over even "as fitted" plans in showing what was actually done. I can't remember which but one ship I modelled according to the plans had a lovely screw device to operate some of the davits but nowhere on any photos could I spot this device so I reluctantly left it off. Anyway I hope you can manage to abstract some gems from my writings over 4 years. I have enjoyed writing these Solutions - I hope you enjoy reading them.

*Brian King 2007*

# 2. Photo Etching for the Clueless

The process of photo etching consists of using an etchant to remove unwanted material from a sheet of metal to produce flat components. Because no physical force is used, shapes of incredible complication can be produced without burrs or distortion and with a very high degree of both dimensional and repetitive accuracy. This enables thick components to be built up from a number of layers thus overcoming one weakness of the process that thin sheets etch better than thick ones owing to "undercutting" by the etchant when thick material is etched. 3D components can be produced if the shape

**Fig 1. The crane fitted to the authors model of HMS Elizabeth, fabricated from photo etched components.**

**Fig 2. An assembly fixture for ladders worked but producing the item from photo etched parts proved far simpler.**

involved can be developed from a 2D shape that can be etched. **Fig.1** shows one of the cranes on my model of HMS Queen Elizabeth. Apart from the pulleys the booms and the tower structure, these are made entirely from etched parts. Another example would be a free-standing ladder with stiles and steps that could be etched flat and folded up to produce an accurate ladder.

Those of us who have tried know how difficult it is to produce an accurate scale ladder from separate pieces even with jigs or fixtures. I remember years ago making an elaborate fixture in aluminium to assemble all the necessary pieces to make a soldered brass ladder only to find it would not work. **Fig.2**. You could not remove the ladder from the fixture. I pondered over this for some time having spent much labour on the fixture. I

finally and regretfully concluded that the expansion of the brass during soldering was the cause, as on cooling the ladder revered to its normal size and the consequent shrinking locked it in the fixture. Eventually I modified the design to suit steps and stiles made of wood which worked satisfactorily if you were sparing with the adhesive otherwise it locked itself in again! Photo etching is far easier.

We in the model boat business have come lately to this technique, which has been embraced by the railway types for a long time. Ship modellers have noticed the inclusion of etched part sheets in all sorts of kits. Plastic injection has limitations in how thin a section it is possible to produce and brass etching fills that gap to provide guard-rails and the like. The etching technique allows very

**Fig 3. A significant nuber of parts used to build this model of the Italian battleship RN Duilio (see**

thin sections to be etched unlike injection moulding. Cardboard models can also be improved for the same reason - material limitations. Cardboard also has strength limitations! Etching also gives the kit manufacturer a method of supplying the kit builder with very accurately made sheet parts - accurate in dimension and in repeatability. Etched parts supplement the 3D parts provided as white metal or resin castings. Here we have touched on one of etching's limitations. Because of the way the process works, thin sheets etch better than thick ones so the method is limited to sheet material. Although brass is the usual material, stainless steel and even aluminium can be etched. Brass, however, suffices for most model jobs. Stainless steel provides a much stronger job but parts are difficult to remove from the

matrix owing to its extra strength.

How does the process work? The principle is that the sheet to be etched has some areas protected (those areas that represent the components) and other areas left bare. The etchant, usually ferric chloride, will then etch away the unprotected areas leaving the components unaffected. The process is akin to the production of printed circuit boards (PCB's) although they have a plastic backing sheet, which is absent in our type of work. Those of you with razor-sharp minds, unlike me, will have twigged that the essence of the system is how do you get the protected areas on to the sheets? Commercial etchers etch from both sides of the sheet, which obviously saves time and enables different patterns to be etched on each side so you need to provide two masks, tools, acetates or whatever you call them. These are transparent sheets with the design printed on them in black. The metal sheet to be etched is cleaned to a condition similar to that required for electroplating. It is then coated with a light sensitive emulsion that is exposed through the appropriate mask using ultra violet (UV) light. Where the UV can penetrate the mask (i.e. the transparent areas) it will not harden the emulsion when it is developed. In areas protected by the mask (i.e. the black areas or components) the emulsion will harden and cannot be washed off. Where the emulsion is removed the etchant can attack the metal of course. That is the principle of photo etching. The details can vary but the use of a "resist", as the hardening emulsion is called, is essential. There are emulsions that react the opposite way in which case the components need to be transparent and the areas to be etched away need to be black.

The whole process can be done at home using the same materials as those sold for PCB work by firms such as Maplins. You can even buy an UV exposure box, which makes determination of the correct exposure of the light sensitive emulsion easier. Using raw daylight can be a bit hit and miss. Usually home etching is a one-sided affair (i.e. only the one side is etched with the reverse protected by paint, tape, etc) owing to the difficulty of accurately lining up the masks either side of the metal sheet. This has two main disadvantages. Etching times will be doubled, as the etchant has to eat through the whole thickness. Double-sided etching only needs to penetrate half thickness. Longer etching times mean more "under-cutting" can take place. This is because the etchant has time to creep back under the resist - obviously this should be avoided. The other disadvantage is that half-depth "fold" lines cannot be produced. With double-sided etching thin "folding" lines can be etched in from either the front or back surfaces. These produce very sharp folds, which are highly desirable. These folding lines are only etched half depth. This is

achieved by only showing them on one mask either the front or back. Cutting lines must appear on both front and back sheets to ensure the etchant cuts right through of course. Although it is possible to do the whole job at home, experience shows the advantages of getting a professional etcher to do the actual etching work. However, your good self can do the production of the artwork, which the etcher uses to make the masks. I started using a drawing board being a draughtsman but those familiar with those awful things called computers can use CAD (computer aided design) to produce extremely accurate artwork both dimensionally and repetitively. To whet your appetite I append a picture of the stern end of my model of the RN Duilio (in this case RN does not stand for Royal Navy but Regia Nave, as she was an Italian battleship). **Fig.3**. In the picture the following parts were etched:

All the guard-rails including those around the two ladderways

The coamings around the ladderways were developed as 2D shapes, etched, folded-up and soldered

To simulate the planking on the deckhouse sides these were made as an appliqué etching with the planks, door and window patterns half-etched in.

The gun mounts and racers

Grids on the aft ventilators

Gratings for the helmsmen

Skylight window frames and protective bars

Stretchers alongside the deckhouse

The nameplate with letters etched proud

Side ports with hinges and rigols

Wheel on the cowl vent

Circular hatches with half etched grid patterns at the extreme aft end

Ship's boats: rudder, thwarts, ribs (timbers), footboards and oars

The main steering wheels and supporting "A" frames were made up of about six laminated etched parts.

The smaller wheel was also made up from laminations.

**Above and Below. The authors model of HMS Glorious made extensive use of photo etched parts.**

# 3. Toolin' up - Jigs

It is always interesting to compare your method of working with fellow model makers. When I read working articles in magazines I often think to myself I wouldn't have done it that way. Rather like the Irishman who, on being asked directions, replies: "I wouldn't have started from here anyway". How one tackles any given job depends on many things: tools available both hand and machine, skill, aptitude and training, or even what you have been used to. One might give examples. The chap without a lathe uses a hand drill clamped in his vice to "turn" his gun barrels. The chap with a lathe probably produces a better job and quicker but needs must when the Devil drives.

Another example might be where engineers have to do some woodwork. The vertical corner posts on the glass display cases that I make have square-sectioned rebates top and bottom to house the top and bottom frames. These rebates can be taken out with normal woodworking tools but a vertical milling machine equipped with a metal-cutting end mill or slot drill does an excellent and probably more accurate job. Well it does for me anyway! This is a case of engineering training being applied to carpentry.

However, one rarely sees the use of special jigs and fixtures in model making described. Production engineering relies on them, of course, but most model makers have no exposure to production engineering and have no such helpful aids in use!

The object of this article is to show how relatively simple jigs and fixtures can help model making enormously.

Firstly we ought to define our terms although in practice the terms are bandied about willy nilly (whoever he was!). A jig is a device for holding the work and guiding the tool. An instance would be a drill jig, which often consists of a box enclosing the work with holes in it to guide the drill bit. For high production the holes are usually fitted with hardened steel bushes to prevent excessive wear. The "box" incorporates a means of accurately locating the job. All this means that parts can be speedily produced with accuracy and without the need for any measurement at all. The accuracy is guaranteed by the design and accuracy of the jig. If that defines a jig a fixture is something that holds the work but does NOT guide the tool. For instance, a milling fixture secures the work to the table of a milling machine in its correct position but the tooling is separate.

To illustrate I describe a jig that can solve one

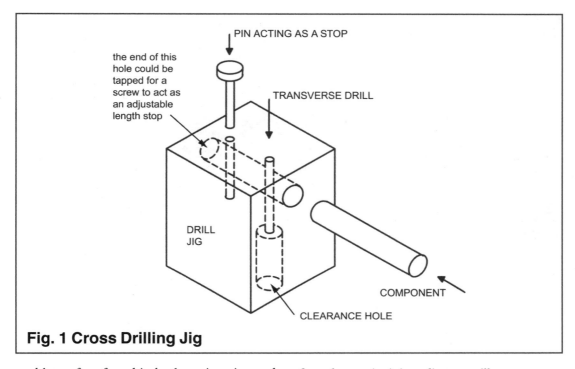

PIN ACTING AS A STOP

the end of this hole could be tapped for a screw to act as an adjustable length stop

TRANSVERSE DRILL

DRILL JIG

COMPONENT

CLEARANCE HOLE

## Fig. 1 Cross Drilling Jig

problem often found in both engineering and model making which is the dreaded transverse hole across a cylindrical rod or bar. You will all have found getting the hole truly across a diameter without breaking the drill or using strong language is difficult - on a bad day you might say impossible! Even for one hole it may be worthwhile making a jig. Firstly consider the problem. The position of the hole from the end should be the easy bit so mark its position. On metal I use a felt-tip pen to colour the surface and then scribe the lines on it. The angular position may not matter but it will if it has to line up with any other features, say other holes, or the bar is shaped, so mark that position and centre punch the intersection of the lines. This can be a problem as, particularly with small rods, the darn centre punch slides of the curve and you mark the wrong place if you get anything at all that is! When you do get it right you can then proceed to drill the hole with the aid of one or two Vee blocks and a drill press. Do not try and freehand drill such holes unless

forced to, as incipient disaster will turn to a broken drill and/or an inaccurate hole - a complete disaster.

Try making the jig shown in **Fig.1**. Find a block of brass or aluminium, but preferably brass, and drill into a hole just large enough to accommodate your rod. You can then very carefully mark out the position of the transverse hole as shown and drill this hole. By leaving the drill in you can sight through the larger hole to see if you have succeeded in getting it truly across the diameter. If you have, you have your jig. If not drill another hole using the error seen in the first hole to get the second one correct. Plug the first hole to avoid mistakes.

Lets examine the result. You have perfect support for both work and drill. In fact the latter is supported along its length and cannot deviate. Really this is the principle of good engineering practice, which is to make the tool and work do what YOU want and not what they (the tool and work) think is easier and they will do if they get half a chance.

**Fig 2. Aimple drilling jig, note the lip arount the edge to facilitate location. Below Fig 3. This jig for drilling ladder rung holes was photo etched.**

There are some further points to consider. If the jig is to work satisfactorily the drill swarf must be able to clear itself. If the holes become blocked with swarf trouble is inevitable; never use blind holes in a jig. Always use a sharp drill and continually ease off the drill; do not try and force it through. In all probability a broken drill will destroy both work and jig. This is an example of a very simple jig which I have even made using a piece of Perspex for the jig body. This will obviously have a limited life but for a few holes it is adequate enough. You will note the removable pin acting as a stop. With it removed the job can be passed through and further holes drilled. If necessary an external stop can be engineered. An alternative, suggested on the drawing, is to put a screw into the remote end of the hole to provide an adjustable stop.

Another relatively simple example of this sort of jig is where a number of holes in a circular pattern or otherwise on a disc (wheel or similar) need to be drilled. To mark out each

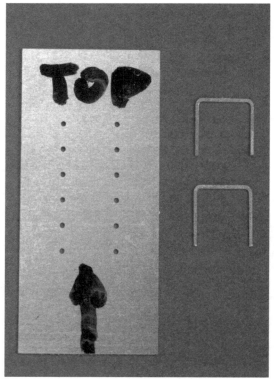

**Fig 4. the holes for the rungs of this ladder are jig drilled and the rungs spaced out evenly by simply inserting a temporary spacer.**

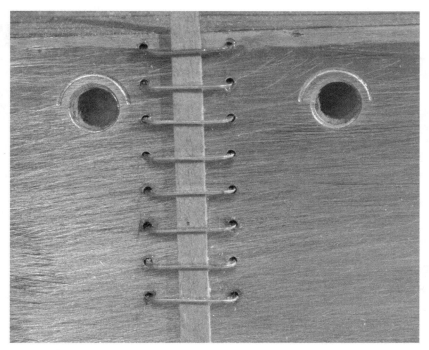

one, if say 40 are required, can be time consuming and very boring. Consider making a simple plate jig locating either on the outside diameter or, if the job has a central hole, locating on that using a spigot on the jig. This can be carefully marked out and drilled and simply dropped on to the job and drilled through. The beauty of this is that the jig can be checked for accuracy and re-made if necessary without scrapping any work. With care all the jobs should be identical and accurate and done in a fraction of the time needed for doing the job from first principles. See **Fig.2** which shows what I mean. Notice the lip on the O/D for location.

A very simple template jig is shown in **Fig.3**. This is to enable the holes to be drilled in the side of a hull for a rung-type ladder. It was an etching produced along with the other etched components. The positional hole accuracy was guaranteed by CAD and so was the shape and accuracy of the etched rungs, two of which are also shown in the photo. **Fig.4** shows the finished ladder. Note the piece of wood that first acted as a depth stop and was left in position to provide protection from an accidental knock.

The point of all this is to open your eyes to the possibilities of extending your expertise. The limit is really your own imagination. Undoubtedly those of us who have been lucky enough (?) to experience production engineering have an advantage when it comes to doing this sort of work but that's life I guess! I haven't got round to fixtures as I intended so I will explain those next.

# 4. Toolin' up - Fixtures

In my last column I intended to write about both jigs and fixtures but the jig section demanded more space than I had catered for so the fixture element was omitted. But before continuing perhaps I need to re-define our terms? You will remember that a jig holds the work and guides the tool whereas a fixture holds the work securely and in the correct position but does not control the tool.

Just to extend your knowledge lets look at a production example. Yes, I know its relevance to the modelling world may be somewhat remote but these columns of mine are not merely to train but to educate. There is a difference!

Consider the problem of machining two parallel flat faces of a block accurately in one pass as shown diagrammatically in **Fig.1**. This shows two milling cutters fixed to an arbour set to the correct width cutting the two parallel faces in one pass. The fixture holds the work in the correct

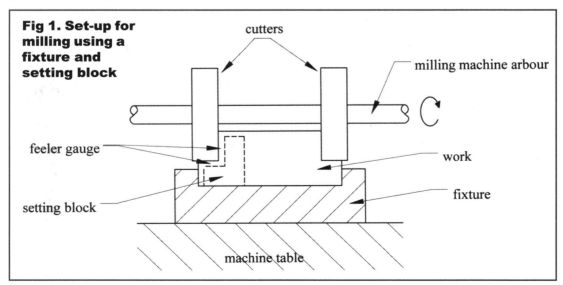

**Fig 1. Set-up for milling using a fixture and setting block**

cutters

milling machine arbour

feeler gauge

setting block

work

fixture

machine table

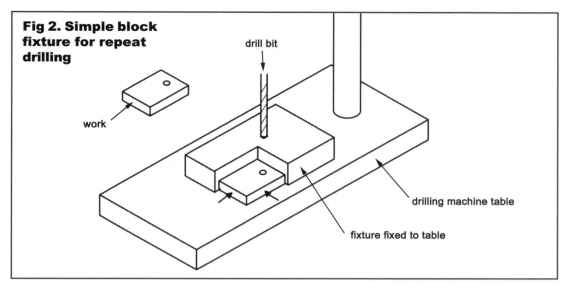

**Fig 2. Simple block fixture for repeat drilling**

drill bit

work

drilling machine table

fixture fixed to table

position relative to the cutters. The dotted block shown provides a vertical and horizontal surface to allow the fixture to be positioned correctly with respect to the cutters. Setting is done by using a feeler gauge just like the one you use for setting spark plug gaps. The setting block is mounted out of the way of the cutters and does not interfere with the cutting action in any way.

That is the principle but how can we apply it to the model world? Drilling the same hole(s) in several identical components often comes up. One way is to mark out each one individually and drill away. Boring and not likely to produce identical results unless your marking out has been done very carefully and the drilling likewise.

A simpler and more accurate way would be to put two stops at right angles on to the table of your drilling machine and use these to "nest" the components whilst drilling them. You need to get the stops, or as we in the trade call them lays, in the correct relationship with the drill bit of course. If you are paying attention you will have been there before me! **Fig.2** shows the idea.

An even simpler example is sanding mitres. I have never got on with mitre boxes and the like for sawing/planing on the 45degree

angles required when building the wooden framework for glass display cases. They never produce the accuracy I require. You need to get tight joints on this type of work otherwise you get murmurs to the effect that the bloke (i.e. me) has lost it!

What I do is to mark out and rough saw the mitres leaving enough on for final sanding to an accurate angle. To do this you need a disc sander with a table. Fix to the table with a "G" clamp a piece of wood large enough to act as a lay. Set this to the correct angle and try sanding the work. Check it for 45 degrees, or any other angle come to that, and adjust the lay as required. It usually does need slight adjustment owing to the "spring" in the system when you shove the work against the revolving sanding disc. You must also ensure that the work remains truly vertical with respect to the table otherwise you will get a compound angle and trouble on assembly.

Not only is this a very accurate way of producing such angles but also produces an excellent surface for gluing. However, I will discuss gluing and adhesives in a later column (if the editor continues to publish them that is!). As I said in my last column you are only limited here by your own imagination. In our book " Photo Etching for Modellers" Azien

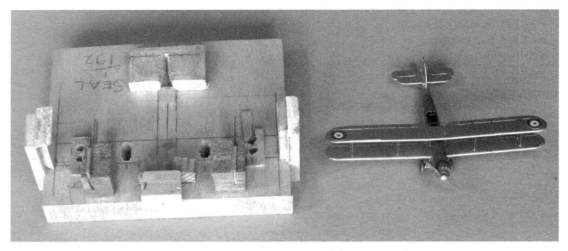

**Fig 3. An assembly fixture helped produce 6 identical aircraft models for HMS Glorious.**

Watkin and I quoted Albert Einstein who said, "Imagination is more important than knowledge". I truly believe that to be so when you are in the business of creating something.

Another use of fixtures is when complicated assemblies are required. A typical example of this aspect of fixtures was the assembly of very small biplanes for my models firstly of HMS Queen Elizabeth and then the aircraft carrier HMS Glorious. In the later case I made 24 miniature aircraft 6 off each of 4 types. These are the kinds of detail that attract the eye and need to be both identical and accurate. They were made largely of brass etchings with a wood fuselage. The problem was assembly and with both upper and lower wings it became a two-stage job. Fixtures or assembly jigs (although that is really the wrong term) were made for all four types. The first requirement was to get the lower wing, fuselage and tail plane in the correct juxtaposition, at right angles etc. A flat wooden base plate was prepared and appropriate lines marked on. Wood blocks were then glued on where necessary to align and support the various pieces. **Fig.3**. The accent was on accuracy. The result may look messy but as it did not become part of the finished model that did not matter to me anyway, as long as it did its designed job. Some modellers would spend time and energy to produce a good-looking fixture but in my book that is unnecessary and a waste of time. But it is your time if you wish to go down that particular path.

With the basics set the fixture was added to, to allow the upper wing to be assembled. The result was 6 identical miniature models but I then had the job of painting them!

Always remember that jigs and fixtures can be checked for accuracy before use and either modified or thrown away but their accuracy determines the final result.

# 5. Press Tooling

The first factory I worked in, in fact served my time in, largely made parts from bar stock, castings and forgings. As the war was on when I started work we were on armaments - such things as 6-pounder guns, aircraft undercarriage legs and fuel injection pumps. All 3D subjects as it were. However, later on in my working life I ended up in a factory that largely made only 2D components mainly with press tools. Lathes of all kinds, milling and drilling machines, etc dominated the first factory. Presses of all kinds dominated the later factory and I came into contact, really for the first time, with press tools and found what they could do. My technical education was largely concerned with the sorts of items manufactured by the first factory so it really was a great new experience.

## Press Tools

The basic parts of a press tool consist of a die (the female part of the tool) and a punch (the male part) that enters the die either to punch out a component or to form a shape of some kind. The actual tools, which do the work, are supported in a structure called a die set, which consists of two machined slabs of, usually, cast iron about 1.5in thick. The lower slab has two or more upright pillars fixed to it. The upper slab slides on these pillars. This structure is a precision assembly that ensures that the punch, fixed to the upper slab, is always in perfect alignment with the die attached to the lower slab. This is essential as any misalignment will "edge" the die or punch and ruin the tool.

What has all this to do with model making

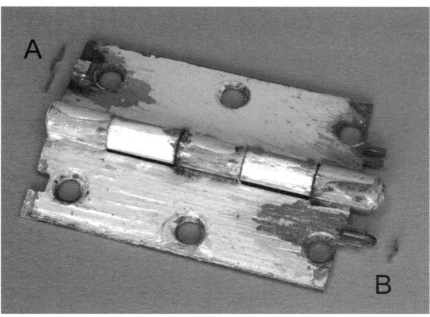

**Fig 1. A simple press tool based on a door hinge produced multiple clips (A & B) for a Victorian warship.**

**Fig 2. Simple press tool in close up to show how the componemt labelled B in Fig 1. is shaped.**

one may well ask. Well it has, as I shall explain. There comes a time when components such as those shown as A and B in **Fig.1** require to be made in appreciable numbers. Now one can sit with pairs of pliers (numerous) and proceed to bore oneself to death bending parts up individually. Result - the aforesaid boredom and a miserable collection of parts none of which really match each other. The component marked B in **Fig.1** was required on one of my Victorian warships being the clip that retained the upper ends of the torpedo net booms into their crutches. About forty were required, including the ones that get lost on the floor! The shape was obviously a press job that would quickly produce the number required and produce the accuracy too.

Obviously a die set and the press to put it in was not to hand so I cast about for a device that consisted of two surfaces that came together accurately and consistently. I suddenly realised that ordinary 3in steel hinges (butts), the kind use to hang doors, could do the job.

**Fig.2** shows how it was shaped to provide a more or less instant press tool, which provided correctly formed accurate clips. In case this is not clear **Fig.3** shows how the tool works.

On one leaf of the hinge a wire of the same diameter as the boom was soldered to form the male part (punch) of the tool whilst a mating slot was made to provide the die part of the deal. The width of these "fingers" was made to enable the "ears" of the component to be trimmed off to the correct overall length. The material used was 0.008in brass shim about 1.5mm wide. A vice was used to clamp up and close the press tool.

Instead of the straight up and down action of a proper press the arcuate (shaped like an arc) action of the hinge means one end (that nearest the hinge pin) traps the material first and allows the material to gather over the die before the other end is finally trapped. Obviously a greater length of material is required to form the clip than just a straight

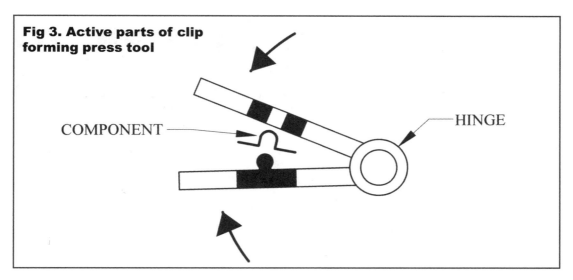

## CHAPTER 5

**Fig 3. Active parts of clip forming press tool**

COMPONENT — HINGE

line measurement. Think about it!

The idea can be used to make "top hat" sections (A in Fig.1), again a shape often required in model work. The other use of this technique is shown in **Fig.4** where it is used to put a joggle into a strip (A is the component, B shows the joggle, C shows the locating pins - note the flat locating edge, and D shows the clearance holes required to clear the pins - C). This is useful if a joint is required but the surface needs to be level. Joining two strips together showing a level surface can also be achieved, of course, by using a butt strap to join the two pieces together but this means you now have three pieces to juggle with instead of two if you use a "joggle". Putting a joggle that is two right-angled bends very close together is impossible without using a tool of this type.

As I have said before the only limitation is your imagination and your skill.

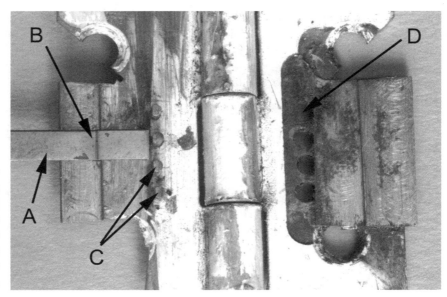

**Fig 4. Slightly more complex press tool using the same principle of a hinge as the basis.**

# 6. Working to Dimensions?

This column is about dimensions as you may guess from the title. But surely a dimension is a dimension is a dimension? Yes and no.

Firstly we modellers do not normally work to a dimension as such. We do not make a part 26.5mm long because a drawing tells us that that is the correct figure. What we actually do is to measure a drawing and that becomes the dimension. The drawing concerned may be 150 years old. During that 150 years it has probably shrunk, stretched or distorted several millimetres particularly if it was originally some nine feet long (some National Maritime Museum original drafts are indeed that length).

All practical engineers of course would never measure a drawing to get a dimension to save their lives. That would go against all their training. The legend printed large on most engineering drawings says: "DO NOT SCALE" and it means what it says. You may say, well the drawing was drawn to scale so why can't you measure the drawing? The reason is that a dimension may have been altered but the drawing was not modified to suit. Drawing office work does not come cheap! Measuring an altered dimension could lead you down the garden path with no problem at all.

We are forced to measure drawings because we have no option. I have been dealing with old Victorian drawings for about 30 years and have come to know the pitfalls (for the modeller) they are likely to contain. I normally build the hull to the lines drawing if I have one. One hopes at least that drawing will be correct and tie up with the transverse section drawing. Before starting to build I always check if the two marry up. For example, check that the beam dimensions at all stations correspond with the appropriate section drawing. If there is trouble here you must get it right before you start cutting material. How you do that is up to you as every case may be different but waterlines and transverse sections MUST tie up.

The next problem is having built the hull does the deck shape you have produced fit the deck plan? If it does you are lucky. I have found that the two shapes, the actual model deck and the appropriate deck plan, often do not agree despite the fact that you have built it to the lines drawing. The difference may not be great but if there is any discrepancy it

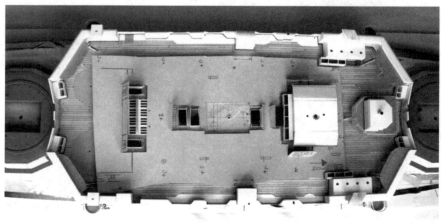

**Fig 1. Cardboard template used to mark position of minor components - dropped over major features.**

**Fig 2. This coloured stripe provides a reference for size and location of features.**

means the position of the deck edge, or near deck edge features, will have to be adjusted.

Getting all the deck clutter in the right place, or as close to the right place as possible can become very difficult. Recently I built an elaborate deckhouse following a detail drawing (these were elaborate plans with all details drawn out) only to find it was about 6mm longer than the same deckhouse shown on the GA (General Arrangement). It was not really possible to cut it down in length as I had clad the outside with simulated planking made from a brass etching. As there was considerable deck clutter at both ends of this deckhouse this presented a considerable problem. In a case like this I spend time examining all the possibilities. With such problems do not rush in only to find there was a better solution. Eventually the solution was to juggle the pieces around to minimise the errors and to hope nobody notices.

This type of problem is not rare in complicated modelling. One tip to remember is to make all parts slightly smaller than scale as I find my components always tend to come out slightly over-size. In many cases this causes no trouble but sometimes you find things are more crowded than the drawing shows and this is nearly always because of the above fault.

Another problem is locating data particularly as straight lines on ships are somewhat of a rarity. The longitudinal centre line is straightforward but lengths are not. Long experience has taught me to ignore bow and stern as datums and to establish a transverse datum somewhere in the centre of the ship, say the centre line of a funnel or mast, and measure from there. Mark your datums on your drawings and stick to them. It is also a good idea to mark your central deck plank with a piece of masking tape. It is all too easy to measure from what you think is the king plank only to find later that it wasn't!

With the main components fitted (such things as deckhouses, funnel bases, etc.) it may be difficult to locate such things as coalholes, eye bolts and ammunition hand-ups. These do tend to get forgotten in the broad scheme of things. To do this I make a cardboard template with the cutouts for the existing main components which enables it to be laid flat onto the deck itself. The position of all these small items can be marked on this template and simply pricked through onto the deck.**Fig.1**. The template can also be carefully checked for accuracy before use to avoid misplaced items and unwanted fixing holes, etc. This is a GOOD THING if you have just spent "n" weeks laying a proper planked deck!

The heights of components are also very important but often forgotten. Great care needs to be taken if, for instance, the ship carries a coloured stripe around the superstructure. This will show up any height errors like a sore thumb. **Fig.2.**

# 7. The Art of the Masque

Twenty-four years ago I wrote an article for an American magazine under the above title. Forgive me for using the same title again but it is too good to waste. At that time I defined it as: masque - a theatrical performance akin to that seen when a modeller removes his masking tape and finds the underlying paint comes off with it or he discovers paint bleed over what should have been an immaculately protected surface. The bright ones amongst you, if anyone bothers to read this that is, will have twigged that I am going to discuss the other type of mask i.e. that used when painting. At that time I thought I knew a bit about the art of masking but despite the fact that you cannot teach an old dog new tricks I have since acquired a few more tips about the subject. Whenever I get to the stage in building a model that requires reaching for the paint pot I get cold feet. This I know is the point when things start to go wrong. This is the point when things turn nasty and I start having bad dreams. Masking is usually required to separate two or more colours or basically to stop paint getting where it isn't wanted. One way of doing this is to spray things separately, preferably off the model, as this requires no masking and produces a 100% guaranteed job. This is not possible all the time; for instance putting the

boot topping on a hull will normally require several stages of masking. **Fig.1**.

**A** the basic grey rectification coat

**B** a strip of white sprayed on with pencil line marking top edge of boot topping

**C** first (false) masking tape applied to "wrong" side of pencil line (see text)

**D** second (proper) masking tape laid to first masking tape

**E** false masking tape removed and black upper hull sprayed

**F** false masking tape applied to reveal width of white boot topping

**G** proper masking tape applied to edge of false tape, which is removed, and red anti-fouling sprayed

**H** masking tape removed to reveal the final result

Firstly always use tape made especially for masking and no other. Masking tape adhesive is less strong than that applied to other kinds of tape. Cellotape for instance has a very powerful adhesive that will pull paint off without a bye your leave or thank you. It can, however, be used on surfaces which are not painted. For instance, if "windows" are to be left on a Perspex item it can be used and is an excellent protector. It has one disadvantage when used as a mask in that it tends to leave

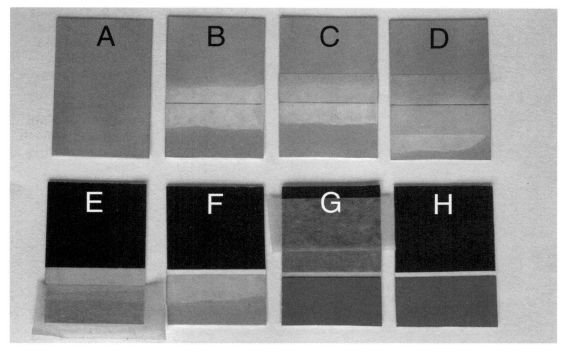

**Fig 1. Step by step masking technique used to produce boot topping white stripe.**

an adhesive residue on the surface. This can be easily removed using a cotton bud soaked in white spirit, not however, after the paint has properly set.

The first job is to plan your masking very carefully. This may sound obvious but it is of the greatest importance. There are often at least a couple of ways of masking a particular job based on which area and which colour goes on first. You often find that one way is far easier than the alternative. In fact you may find that one way produces a headache of a job when trying to mask for the subsequent coat(s). The sort of problem I mean, is having to mask very close to an object or a bend. This is where the natural strength of the tape overcomes its adhesive powers and it fails to seal its defining edge however hard you try to rub it down. You then get problem number two - paint bleed. For those not fully awake this is where the paint penetrates the edge seal and you perform the above masque.

Problem number one is paint rip off. This occurs when the underlying paint has a greater affinity for the tape than it has for its substrate. Really a case of misguided love. We get it everywhere! The answer to this is correct technique. You must ensure that the paint's adhesion to its substrate (the surface it is on) is as perfect as possible. The points to watch are as follows:

1. Make sure the surface is very clean with no residual grease, and that includes finger grease, or dust.

2. Use a primer. Do not expect a heavy coat of glossy paint or enamel to adhere well without a primer. They were not designed for that purpose. Spray or brush your primer on thinly. You should still be able to see the original surface through the paint. This thin coat should adhere very well even on aluminium and dural both metals notoriously difficult when it comes to paint adhesion. If possible leave this first coat for 24hrs before

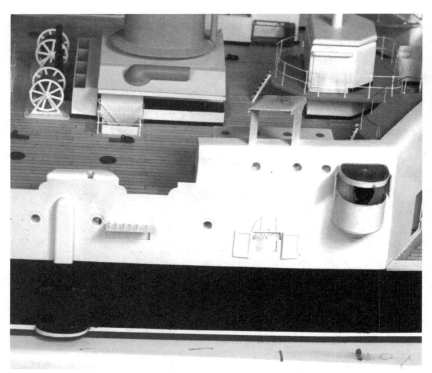

**Fig 2. The boot topping white stripe on HMS Camperdow. Opposite page - Fig 3. camouflage pattern of HMS Queen Elizabeth is a demanding task.**

continuing the paint job. If it is white (or another light colour) you may need to build up opacity before the final coat. But put no more paint on the job than is necessary. Thick paint hides detail and should therefore be avoided. Thick coats tend to gang up together and lose their affinity with the primer. In other words they peel off.

## Masking Technique

Having got the basic coat on properly what of the actual masking technique? I suppose the first problem is to select the masking tape to use. I find the brown paper tape marketed under the name of BETTO (Chinese I believe) excellent. This can be obtained in various widths and I have never had trouble with it except with age when the adhesive tends to leave itself on the job, which can be a nuisance. If you want to ensure the cleanest line lay a length onto a clean piece of plastic and re-cut the edge.

More expensive masking tape by Tamiya is sold in a plastic container and it therefore retains a cleaner edge. Neither of these tapes is flexible (i.e. corrugated) and it therefore needs skill to negotiate it around curves. You usually need a line to lay the tape to. However, I find laying to a line difficult. My technique is to lay a piece of tape on the side of the line that is to be painted - the reverse of what you would normally expect. This tape can be re-laid as many times as is required until you get a fair run. View it from all angles until you are satisfied that it is perfect and that it meets up correctly with the other side of the hull if, for instance, it is marking the waterline.

With this in place you lay the "proper" tape to it and remove the first piece and discard it as you may have worn out its adhesive. Rub down the defining edge hard. I use a piece of end grain balsa for this or a soft rubber which will remove any remnant of pencil line, etc.

## CHAPTER 7

Make sure the first tape has not left any adhesive residue that, if not removed, will be incorporated into the subsequent paint!

On nearly completed models requiring touch-up spraying, over-spray can be a real problem. I use cloths draped over the model, which are very effective as well as pieces of tape of course. Other nooks and crannies can be filled with dampened toilet tissue, which will accommodate itself well to the odd shapes you find on boats and the like. When masking is complete re-check your defining edge to be sure it is still rubbed down hard and apply the first coat. Keep this as "dry" and mean as possible. The object being to seal the edge of the tape before a heavier coat is applied. Do not expect the seal to withstand a gale force jet of paint and not leak. Yes I know you want to see how it looks but restrain yourself – patience is the name of the game here, as in all high class model making. **Fig.2** shows my partly

completed waterline model of HMS Camperdown with the typical Victorian narrow boot topping and **Fig.3** shows an elaborate example of masking and painting of camouflage on HMS Queen Elizabeth. The whole process must be carried out carefully and properly if you want the best result and to avoid disappointments.

## To conclude a few tips

1. Do not leave masking tape on any longer than is necessary. It can form unwelcome attachments.
2. Keep masked-up models out of the sun to avoid cooking the adhesive. If it does cook you will need a chipping hammer to remove it!
3. Do not pull off the tape at right angles to the surface but pull it off back on itself so that the edge of the tape has a chance to cut the paint film.
4. Keep dust to a minimum.

# 8. Acquiring a Finish

I suppose the one thing that has improved enormously during my lifetime in the modelling guild is the finishing of models. Of course geometric accuracy and fidelity to prototype have also improved but I feel the greatest improvement is in the finish. Some of this is due to better materials of course. Before WWII we had oil bound paints and enamels that dried by oxidising the linseed oil used as a medium and very little else. During the war the paint available, if we were lucky, had dubious parentage and you were lucky sometimes if it dried properly at all!

We still have "oil" paints and enamels but they are much improved on the pre-war versions, the chemistry being entirely different. We now also have water-based acrylics to play with that, in my book, are an improvement on paints and enamels in many ways.

However, perhaps we should first look at the philosophy, as it were, of finishing a model. Much depends on the substrate, the surface onto which the finish is applied. Metals and plastics are relatively easy especially if the dust problem can be solved but more of that later. Wood is a different proposition owing to its grain. If varnish of one type or another is used, finishing decks for instance, not much of a problem exists but if a smooth surface simulating steel is required, problems do exist. When I first became interested in not only my own modelling but also what others were doing I was presented with the "84 coat" brigade as I mentally termed them. This

**Fig 1 & 2 (facing page) Two models finished using aerosol spray paint that does produce excellent results if properly applied.**

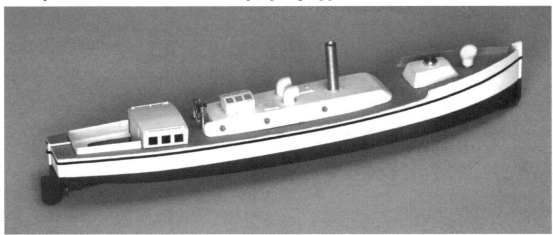

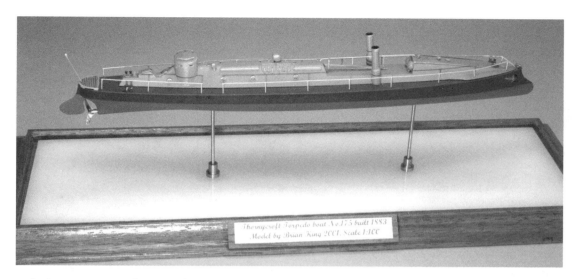

Thornycroft Torpedo boat No.175 built 1883
Model by Brian King 2001, Scale 1:100

technique was to apply coat after coat of paint, waiting for each coat to harden before rubbing down to finally produce a near perfect glassy gloss finish much admired by all. To my juvenile mind even then it didn't seem the right way to tackle the job. Woods do present a difficult surface to work up and some are worse than others having a multiplicity of grain pits that perversely refuse to fill up to present you with a smooth surface.

Perhaps the "84 coat" brigade had no alternative but to build up the finish with many coats of paint but it seemed all wrong to me. To start with it took a great deal of time, always a most precious commodity especially if you are approaching the "sear and yellow" stage of your life. Many coats of paint also spell the exit of fine detail; clogged internal corners and external corners rubbed away with the required rubbing down. Standing back from the problem the requirement of the paint is to colour the surface and provide the wanted degree of "shine" i.e. matt, eggshell or gloss. It should not be required, or used, as surface filler because we have better materials for that job. The Fine Surface Polyfilla sold in a tube is excellent filler for minor blemishes. I notice it seems to adhere to everything. It is white in colour and dries very fast. It can be easily

sanded or cut down with an edge tool. It cannot be used for deep holes as it will not dry out properly but Isopon (David's P38) can be used instead as it sets by chemical action rather than by just drying out.

The secret is in what I call the rectification coat, that is the first overall coat that should show up all the blemishes, excess adhesive, open joints, etc. that may be perfectly secure but would show as a blemish under subsequent coats. The trick is to avoid putting on a thick coat first and covering up the consequent mess. It has been done!

The whole aim is to get the surface ready for the final coat(s) without expecting these final coats to provide the surface. In a perfect world you should only need one rectification coat but I find that I usually need about three attempts before "her in charge of the dockyard" will pass the job. However tiresome this procedure is, and sometimes you feel it will never be good enough, it is what makes the model. Never skimp on rectification.

If your technique is up to it, rubbing down can be reduced to an absolute minimum. I rarely rub down at all at the painting stage. I never try and paint until the required surface has been established. That first depends on the selection of appropriate materials. OK use wood if you must but be prepared to have

**Fig 3. This model also used aerosol spray paint to achieve an excellent finish. Facing page. Authors model of Scillonian gig. Clinker hull provided a painting challenge.**

to work up the surface first as I have explained before any paint is applied. Assuming that you have a "surface" never apply paint with brush, aerosol or airbrush until you have dusted the aforesaid surface with a brush that you keep for that job. This is to remove the dust that will be on the surface whether you can see it or not. You must learn that dust is everywhere and is all to keen to join the party by combining with any paint film you care to lay down. This is where the necessity for rubbing down largely comes from. Another source of "bits" is the skinning over of "oil" paints and enamels, which require the paint to be strained. (Where we are to get old tights material for that job I know not, now that the universal female uniform comprises trousers in some form or other). It always amuses me after finishing a model as to where all the problems have gone? Certainly rectification can be one of those problems but no sign of them should exist at completion: stolen away like the morning mist.

Over the years I have had correspondence regarding the deck colour on WWII warships. The fact of the matter is that whereas we often know the hull camouflage colours with some certainty (my HMS Queen Elizabeth was matched to paint chips) the colour treatment of the decks is unknown. Painted steel was usually dark grey or black, Corticene was chocolate brown (I use Humbrol No.84 matt, which is a close approximation), Semtex varied from pale cream to a medium grey and sometimes red oxide was used. However, I am afraid that worrying too much about the exact shades of ship's paints is rather a waste of time. The fact is we do not know what was available and according to hearsay it largely depended in many cases in what was in the paint store at the time as the paint was mixed from base and powders on board. I had a query recently about the exact colours used on Victorian battleships. Firstly we just do not know and, how the Dickens does one define a given colour? Unfortunately nobody had the forethought to leave us paint chips and to tell us whether they were faded or not!

**Figs.1-3** show examples of good aerosol-sprayed finishes on three ship's boats built for my model of HMS Camperdown. Figs.1 and 2 have solid wood hulls whereas Fig.3 was made from an ABS moulding. The steam picket boat in Fig.1 is 5.7in long, the torpedo boat in Fig.2 is 7in long and the steam pinnace in Fig.3 is just under 4in long.

## CHAPTER 8

# 9. The Black Art of Soldering

In my first column the editor and I asked for ideas for discussion. We had two replies. Fred Graham asked a whole lot of questions regarding steam. I am not a steam freak and my knowledge of the subject is basic, to say the least, although I have built engines and boilers it is just not my scene. I used to run a model engineers class in my technical college and I was about the only one not interested in steam. The other suggestion came from Nick

Hawkins and was basically about soft soldering delicate articles and how the neat unpainted brass ventilator cowls seen on shipping models that used to adorn shipping offices and museums were made.

The answer to the last query is probably by electrolysis. In a book called The Model Ship Builder's Manual of Fittings by Captain A D Isard (Faber and Faber Ltd) and first published in 1939 (and presumably long out

**Fig 1. HMS Camperdowns ships boats are supported on a skid deck. Soldered fabrication shown here before painting.**

of print) he describes the method of electro-plating a pre-cast lead shape to a thickness great enough to be self sustaining after the lead had been melted out. It seemed a very long-winded and complicated process of which I, nor any friend of mine, have any experience. A book on electro-plating would point you in the right direction but you would need to set up an electro-plating bath. This was no problem for those model makers as they tended to plate all sorts of parts: guns, capstans, bollards, etc. all of which look pretty daft to us, especially where the silver plating has tarnished to a dirty black!

## Soft Soldering

I learned how to solder as an apprentice largely making up copper pipe work for test rigs. This, at least, gave me a feel for the process but it was a far cry from the sort of soldering required on the type of model that I build today. **Fig.1** shows the unpainted skid deck that supports the ship's boats on my model of HMS Camperdown. All the joints were soft soldered.

To start at the beginning, we must have:
1. Adequate heat.
2. Cleanliness to a very high degree.
3. An efficient flux and 4. suitable solder.
These are the essentials and how we combine them is open to choice. I have tried several techniques and they all work if you get them right and that usually means after practice.

## Heat

How you provide the heat is up to you with due regard to the job. I normally use a 25watt electric soldering iron, which is adequate for most work but I also use a 75watt iron for heat-hungry jobs. Trying to solder without an adequate heat supply is a doomed endeavour. A big iron is also useful if you want to get a

**Fig 2. The mast of HMS Belfast has multitude of components and the soldering of such an assembly requires careful planning**

lot of heat energy into a job in the shortest possible time to avoid unsoldering a nearby joint. On some jobs a flame is better as no physical contact with the work is necessary. I use a normal DIY butane type. Remember the hottest part of the flame is at the tip of the blue cone.

## Cleanliness

Cleanliness must be in the order of that required for plating. You need to establish an intermolecular bond between base metal and solder or, as we engineering types call it, the solder must "wet" or "tin" the surface. If it refuses to do so and "balls" up, forget it and re-clean the surface. This also applies to the tip of the iron. If a surface refuses to wet the cause may be lack of heat rather than dirt. Experience will quickly teach which is the cause.

## Flux

There are two types of flux: passive and active. On copper and brass we normally use a passive type resin such as Fluxite. On steel we need an active flux such as "Baker's fluid" or zinc chloride (killed spirits). Both types need to be removed before painting especially the active ones as they can continue to be corrosive. I normally wash off with cold water and immerse in a weak solution of detergent to kill any further action. Even if you are using a passive flux a touch of Baker's fluid helps the solder flow enormously.

## Solder

Although some authorities suggest using soft solder alloys other than the standard electrical 60/40 resin filled tin/lead alloy I have never found it necessary so to do. Tinman's solder, sold in sticks can be used but this is un-cored and will require external fluxing.

Solder paste or cream is also available and this is a liquid/paste of solder powder and flux. It can be applied with a brush or cotton bud before any heat is added, which enables the correct amount to be judged and prevents "blobbing". This advantage is offset by its

**Fig 3. Typical "helping hands" device with fitted magnifying glass is a boon for soldering small assemblies.**

expense and that the liquid tends to dry out and become more or less useless. Also if you do not apply heat for long enough to melt all the powder you end up with a mess needing to be cleaned off. However, paste does help the inexperienced in enabling limited amounts of solder to be applied. Excess solder can ruin a job and having to use mechanical methods to remove it i.e. chipping hammers, does tend to wreck delicate etching work! Even files can cause havoc.

## Technique

Having dealt with the basics I will devote the rest of this column to cunning schemes to actually do the soldering. The received way to make a soldered joint is to tin both surfaces, bring them together and apply enough heat to melt the two surfaces together. Well that's the way I was taught. You can ignore the tinning bit and apply the solder to a ready-made clean joint and hope the solder tins and does the job in one stage as it were. Given the surfaces are clean and the flux in the solder and/or the extra flux applied does its job the joint should be satisfactory. The main problem here is you may get too much solder on the joint.

Excess solder, either at the tinning stage or on completion of the joint, can be removed using gravity to allow the solder to flow back onto the iron. Whilst tinning, a piece of wood closely following the iron will remove surplus molten solder. Copper braid is sold that will capillary up excess solder and solder pumps are also available but I find they are not really necessary. If you use the gravity process it is usually followed by a wrist flick to rid the iron of the excess solder. For some totally unaccountable reason the distaff side do not like blobs of solder in their carpets so beware where you use this wrist flick.

## The three on two off phenomenon

Soldering jobs such as **Fig.2** which is the mast of our beloved HMS Belfast now slumbering in the Pool of London requires, to say the least, planning. The sequence must be correct otherwise the three on two off becomes a nightmare reality. Work out which joints will require the most heat i.e. those where most metal is concentrated and do those first. These can be followed by the "lesser" joints. Use heat sinks to absorb heat and to protect established joints. These can be metal clips or anything that will absorb heat and prevent it reaching and unsoldering already made joints. These will only have a limited life however. What I mean by that is if the whole job starts to become hot their protective powers will cease as they themselves will become hot. So quench out. I have used a raw potato as a

heat sink and this works well for really difficult jobs. If it all goes wrong you can always eat the chips!

Always remember that you can still glue in components if necessary.

One problem I have not mentioned is over-heating of the iron. The iron must normally run at a higher temperature than that of the melting point of the solder but this can lead to oxidation of the iron's tinning. In my book Advanced Ship Modelling (Special Interests Model Books) I describe a home-made temperature controller for a soldering iron that I use but space forbids a description here. Three further points need to be made:

1. When etching or making parts that will have to fit together try to design in a mechanical fixing as well, as it makes soldering a doddle.

2. For parts fitted at an angle but still in one plane try pinning these down onto, preferably, a refractory block. These are available from Proops and the like. You can use wood but the scorching produces carbon residues which can contaminate the joint.

3. For difficult compound angle joints "Helping Hands" is a boon. **Fig.3**. Incidentally for those difficult joints it pays to spend a great deal of time on setting up and getting everything properly tinned. A flame is probably best here rather than an iron which may disturb the joint. Getting it right first time eliminates having to break it down, clean it and re-solder. This just wastes time and your patience!

## Resistance Soldering Machines

These are electrical devices that produce low voltage but high current pulses big enough to melt solder. I have one but for the kind of work I do I have never found it useful.

# 10. Lathe Problems

So that we all know what we are talking about **Fig.1** shows a lathe with the parts labelled. I first got my hands on a lathe when I was about 15 and five years after that I was earning my bread on a Myford ML7 making parts for the experimental department in which I was working. My own lathe is now a later version of that Myford and, despite some opinions by "experts" to the contrary; I consider it a first class lathe for model work. Its one disadvantage is low maximum speed due to its plain bearings. I have increased the maximum speed on mine to about 1000RPM, which is as fast as its bearings will allow (the maximum speed was increased by fitting a larger motor pulley).

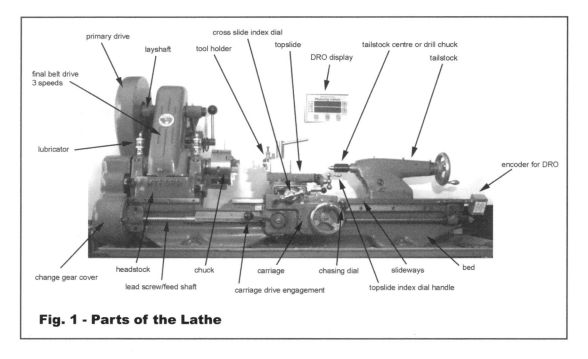

**Fig. 1 - Parts of the Lathe**

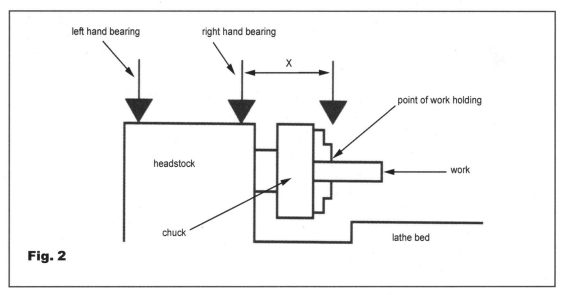

**Fig. 2**

Sooner or later most serious modellers will acquire a lathe but without some training its usefulness will be limited. There is not enough space in this column to cover all aspects of lathe work (there are plenty of books available on that subject) but some points on lathe design and setting-up we can consider.

Firstly, any machinery requires rigidity. Industrial machine tools are usually made of cast iron, which is heavy, rigid and absorbs vibration well. These are the qualities required. However, most modellers' machines are made from lighter materials and therefore lack the most important aspect of machine tool design. They work but are limited in the amount of material that can be removed, but for light work they are probably adequate.

Another factor giving the all-important rigidity is the closeness, or otherwise, of the "point of work holding" to the right hand headstock bearing. **Fig.2** shows what I mean. The dimension "X" should be as small as possible. The reason for this is that the right hand bearing contributes a great deal to the rigidity of the lathe. If the "point of work holding" is miles away from its support you will never achieve smooth and accurate machining.

In my opinion some miniature lathes certainly have the "X" dimension far too big. Careful detail design could have reduced this dimension and made a much better lathe.

## Speeds and Feeds

One problem the beginner has is knowing what speeds to use; presuming the machine has a range of speeds that is. Three things determine the correct cutting speeds:

1. The diameter of the work being machined
2. The material being cut
3. The cutting tool material

I append a table showing the correct cutting speeds when using high-speed steel (HSS) tooling bits for various materials in both Imperial and metric units.

| Material | Cutting Speeds | |
|---|---|---|
| | ft/min | m/min |
| Mild steel | 80 | 24 |
| High carbon steel | 50 | 15 |
| Cast iron | 70 | 21 |
| Brass | 220 | 67 |
| Bronze | 60 | 18 |
| Aluminium | up to 1000 | 305 |

If the diameter of the work is known applying the following formula will give the revolutions to use:
Imperial units: $N = (S \times 12)/(p \times D)$
Where: S cutting speed in ft/min, D = diameter of work in inches, N = revs/min
SI units: $N = (S \times 1000)/(p \times D)$

**Above: Trepanning the circular base from Tufnol for a turret on Bouvet.**

Where: S cutting speed in metres/min, D = diameter of work in mm, N = revs/min
When using Imperial units and machining mild steel a quick way of estimating machine speed is to simplify the formula thus:
(S x 12)/(p x D) assuming p is about 3 and S is 80 it can be reduced to:
(80 x 12)/(3 x D) = (80 x 4)/D = 320/D
So when machining mild steel simply divide 320 by the diameter of the work to get the correct speed. Even I can do that in my head! Note this calculation need not be exact; you can only set the lathe to its nearest available speed anyway! For reasonable tool life do not exceed the cutting speed. Incidentally do not spend money on sophisticated tungsten carbide tipped tools either of the brazed or inserted types. I do not possess any. For all normal work in the modellers' workshop with the low powered machines available ordinary HSS tools are more than sufficient. The exception to this is if a lot of sand

castings with chilled skins are to be machined but that is straying into model engineering, smelly locomotives and the like! It pays to work out the correct speeds as long experience with students has taught me that left to their own devices they always run machines too fast and then complain that their tools blunt too quickly. This misjudgement of correct machine speeds is worse when machining much larger diameter work than that you are used to. It is surprising how slow 6in diameter work needs to turn to avoid exceeding 80ft/min!

## Second Hand?

If you are contemplating buying a second hand lathe try and take someone who is a machinist with you and get his opinion. If that is not possible take a good general look at the machine and note its overall condition. This should give you a good idea of how it has been treated. Get hold of the chuck and see if there is any movement in the aforesaid headstock bearings. If there is this machine is best left alone unless the bearings can be adjusted. Look at the condition of the surface of the bed particularly around the chuck area. If this shows saw cuts and damage this lathe has been badly used. Check if the jaws of the chuck are bell mouthed because if so you will have difficulty in holding some jobs! Also examine the interior taper on the tailstock quill to make sure the female Morse taper is not badly scored. Holding Morse tapered items, drills, drill chucks, etc accurately and without slip depends on the state of this taper.

Check all the gears to see whether they have teeth missing or other damage. This particularly applies to the back gearing situated behind the chuck. Back gearing introduces a subsidiary shaft to allow very slow chuck RPM. If the lathe is equipped with a set of change gears which provide a drive coupling the lead screw/feed shaft to the main spindle check that these are all there and undamaged. If the lathe is more sophisticated and has a Norton gearbox fitted to the left-hand end of the lead screw/feed shaft check that this also works. The function of this box and the change gears is to enable the speed of the lead screw to be changed for screw cutting work. The name Norton does not come from the well beloved Norton motorcycle company but from the great American machine tool company of that name.

# 11. Odds and Sods

I have been thinking of a number of things lately that are worth a mention. For instance there are two kinds of tools we can use which are not really well known.

Rifflers are special files, originally made for die sinkers, which can be used for all sorts of modelling work. As can be seen from **Fig.1** they are usually double-ended with integral handles set between the working ends. You really need a set of shapes and both coarse and fine grades to do the job properly. For some jobs they really are indispensable, e.g. working on all the sorts of curves you get in model making, well I do anyway! You wonder how you managed without them! As I say they were made for work on dies which, being largely female in shape, have a great number of concave surfaces to smooth and polish.

The kind of modelling that I try to do, sometimes successfully, requires a large number of small holes to be drilled. I try not to drill holes below 0.5mm diameter as below this size drilling becomes ever more difficult owing to the delicacy of the drills. Holding (driving) them is also difficult unless you have a really good collet. Incidentally three-jaw collets are better than the four-jaw type. They are usually more expensive as they require three cuts and

not two to produce. Think about it! If you have a good collet that will grip your smallest drills keep it for that purpose only and do not wear it out on larger drills.

In "normal" engineering you rarely get holes more than about two diameters deep. This causes no swarf problems. Deeper holes usually require swarf clearance otherwise there is a danger of the drill binding in the hole and possibly breaking. This problem is alleviated in industry by the use of coolant either water based or oil based. We modellers do not use coolant so all one can do is to frequently relieve the drill to clear the swarf. This is OK for metal as the swarf usually clears itself fairly readily.

When drilling Perspex or similar thermoplastic plastic, however, the swarf does not clear as it usually melts and sticks to the drill itself. The reason for melting is that the drill heats up and being tiny there is little metal to absorb the heat. I have never solved this problem completely.

There are two ways to tackle the problem: drill very slowly and remove the drill from the hole frequently to remove the un-melted swarf, and apply small amounts of water to the drilling area. Neither of these is really the answer. Another way that gets round the

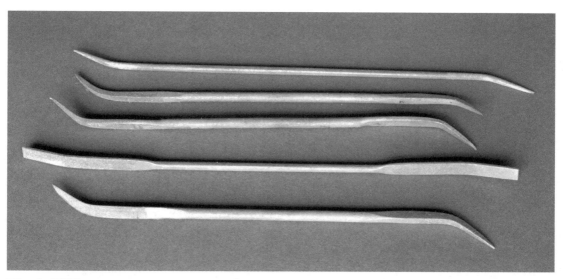

**Fig 1. Rifflers are a very useful model makers tool and are available in a variety of cuts and shapes.**

problem without solving it is to avoid deep small diameter holes by counter-boring at least some of the depth with a much larger drill. This counter-boring can be from either end of the bore or from both ends. The object is to reduce to a minimum the small bore hole length if you follow me. If you don't please read this again. These very small drills can be obtained in little sliding plastic cases that allow extraction of one drill at a time. Buy a couple of packs and cannibalise one to keep the other topped up so that you always have one complete set. Some drills have black or gold coatings. These are either anti-friction or corrosion resistant plating. Allied to the hole problem is control of size. Normally the above packs hold sets of drills 0.1mm difference in size. For all those elderly types like me this is equal to four Imperial thousandths i.e. 0.004in. A very small amount you think but with very small drills 0.004in affects the fit enormously. Obviously drilling out with the next sized drill will probably produce a fit like a lamb's tail down a well. You note the argot you learn in the days of your apprenticeship lasts a lifetime! So, if you were trained properly, do the skills you picked

up then we hope.

The solution to this easing out of holes is a set of watchmaker's (clockmaker's) broaches. **Fig.2.** These look like old-fashioned hatpins. The body consists of a slow-tapered square section topped by a plastic handle. You insert them into the hole and twiddle them whereupon the square corners scrape out the bore. These are essentially tools for removing very small amounts of material but they provide the ideal tool for sizing small bores up to say about 3mm diameter. Like rifflers I find them essential tools for my kind of work. Both these tools are not very well known but are not difficult to obtain from trade stands at model and engineering exhibitions.

The other thing that I thought worth mentioning is the use of a lathe for spraying cylindrical items such as gun barrels. Spraying such items along their length and then turning them before spraying another strip often produces a very poor result.

Try mounting them in the chuck or between centres, whichever suits the shape of the object, run the lathe at about its slowest direct speed and spray with left to right movement.

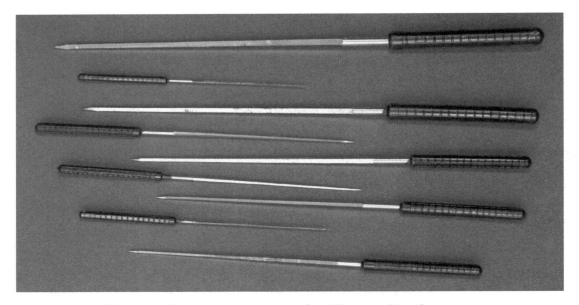

**Fig 2. Swiss files of all types are a more familiar tool to the average modeller.**

It is best to use several passes rather than try and achieve a full coat with one traverse. If you observe the paint film it should not heap up which indicates too much paint is going on. If this happens wipe off the paint and try again but move your spray faster. I am envisaging using an aerosol spray can for this. If you are using an airbrush you may need to run the lathe in back gear as the airbrush may not give enough output. A brush can also be used but if you are using acrylics they do not like being "worked" more than the minimum

**Below: A pin vice and set of collets are very useful for holding both very small drills and components.**

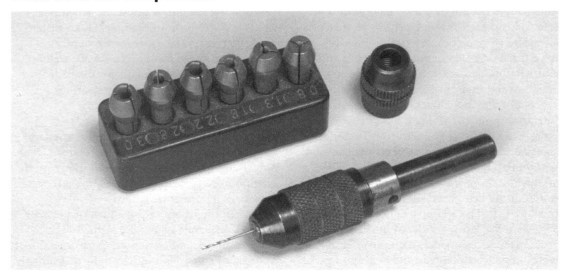

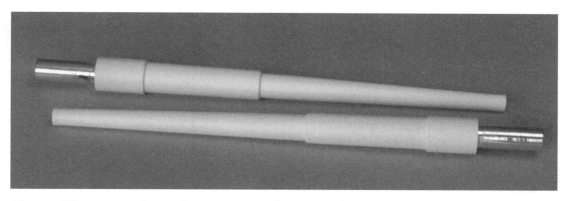

## CHAPTER 11

**Above: These gun barrels were spun in the lathe whilst aerosol sprayed to achieve the incredibly even finish**

and you may find that the paint starts to dry too soon. After spraying continue to run the lathe until the paint has flashed off and, if the lathe has a lamp, applying gentle heat from it will do no harm.

You will need to protect the lathe at least if you are spraying. Cover the bed with paper and put discs of card either end of the work to avoid coating the chuck, tailstock, etc. One final note of caution - if you run the lathe too fast you may get paint thrown back at you! The lathe can also be used with a brush to put black bands on masts and yards, etc. In this case very slow (back gear) speeds are best. I recently used this technique to paint just the top surface of the two capstans on my model. This method is analogous to that used by pottery artists to put gold bands on cups and plates. Finally remember always; pre-dust immediately before painting!

# 12. Davits

Sometimes one sees a model where the detailing lets down the rest of the model and sometimes vice versa. The truth is that on a first class model the attention to the deck clutter and details in general must also be first class. I intend therefore to devote a few columns to various aspects of the smaller features on scale models. As I concentrate on warships some personal bias may be obvious but the principles of good modelling apply to all kinds of modelling marine or otherwise. In this column I am going to discuss davits, which can be a problem. Unfortunately nearly all davits are tapered and that problem needs to be tackled - leaving them of constant diameter is just not on. To start with it looks terrible and marks you out as a beginner. I make mine out of Sif bronze welding wire or brass. Usually the diameter is not large enough to attempt to turn on the taper.

**Fig 1. A wooden support block being used in conjunction with a file to taper material for davits.**

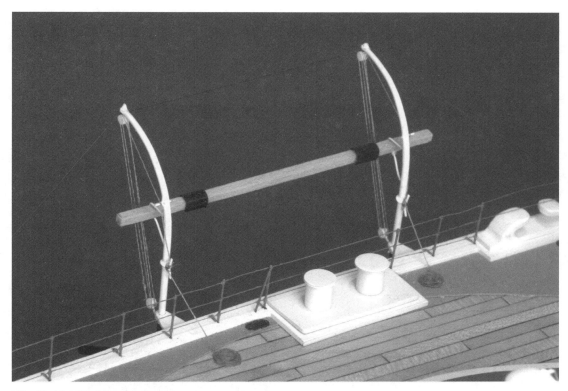

**Fig 2. Radial type davits.**

One way of putting on the taper is to use a special wood block as shown in **Fig.1**. As can be seen a series of different sized tapered grooves have been cut into the block. The taper on the grooves is necessary because the degree of taper on the davit varies. If a suitable length of wire or rod is held in some kind of pin chuck (or the like) it can be placed in a suitable sized groove and a hand file applied. The chuck is necessary to control the wire and rotate it under the file to avoid filing on a series of flats. Use a coarse file first to remove the bulk of the material. Finer files can then be used to bring up a finish followed by emery cloth. I find the worse problem is to get consistency in shape if a number are required. You can partly overcome this by making matching pairs. Differences between pairs sited at different places on the model are not really noticeable!

Bending them up to shape should be able to be done cold. Anneal if you must. Heat to red heat and quench in cold water for convenience but the speed of cooling is not important. If the tip needs flattening it can be done by filing, hammering or squeezing in a vice but do anneal before attempting to drill a hole. The two previous operations will certainly have work-hardened the metal, which makes hard work for the drill! In this case only local annealing needs to be done of course. Aluminium (or Dural) can be used of course but it does not file as well as brass or bronze and cannot be easily soldered if riving spar brackets, or anything else come to that, need to be attached. For those not in the know riving spars are horizontal round, or square sectioned, bars that stop the boat suspended in the davits from swinging about. They usually have at least two bands of cushioning material wrapped around them to protect the boat. In addition two outside canvas straps, arranged diagonally, secure the boat against these protective bands to avoid any movement.

These davits are relatively simple and uncomplicated. **Fig.2** shows an example of the radial type. **Fig.3** shows a complicated davit as fitted on the Italian battleship RN Duilio. The originals must have been castings, probably steel and not cast iron. As can be seen the upper part is "H" section whereas the lower end I made as a turning including the worm wheel. These davits were rotated "out" and "in" board by turning a worm supported in a bracket operating the aforesaid worm wheel. This mechanism is self-locking, as the worm wheel cannot drive the worm. The "H" section part I made from three etched parts soldered together and finally soldered to the turned lower part.

**Fig.4** shows an anchor davit as fitted to Victorian warships. Because the Victorians did

**Right: Fig 3. A more complex davit as fitted to Duilio. Below Finished anchor davits typical of Victorian warships.**

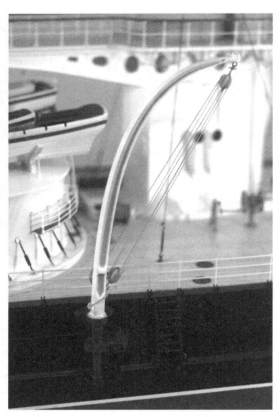

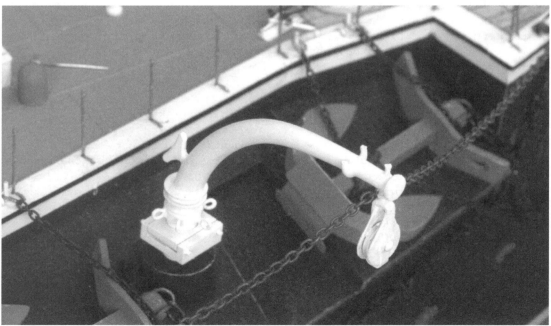

## CHAPTER 12

**Fig 5. Victorian anchor davits in unfinished state. Note the hinge enabling the davits to be stowed flat on deck.**

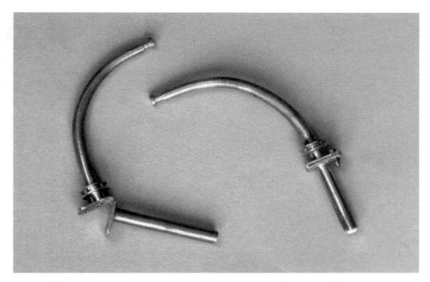

not use stockless anchors, as did later battleships they could not be drawn into the hawse holes but had to be laid onto special sloping anchor beds and secured by quick release mechanisms thereto. Getting these heavy anchors up from the deep and secured required immense effort. The anchors were fitted with a gravity band on their shanks to enable them to be lifted horizontally by the father and mother of all davits as shown. To enable the decks to be cleared for action these giants could be laid flat as they incorporated a hinge near their base. **Fig.5** shows two of these unpainted davits. The left hand one clearly shows this hinge.

The taper on these can usually be turned. The problem is putting in the curved shape, which always requires careful annealing as already described if you make them in brass. If made in copper, a more ductile material, you can usually get away without annealing however, if when bending sudden resistance is felt, anneal before a fracture occurs.

When bending up, owing to their big taper the bend will always occur at the thin end first. Oppose this wilful behaviour and concentrate your efforts on the thick end; the thin end can look after itself. It is always best to draw a template of the curve required so as to have a standard to work to. This sometimes can be drawn from the first one made when you are satisfied with its shape. When tackling difficult bending jobs try and leave enough material at the large end to hold on to in a vice or whatever. Also putting a pipe over most of the smaller end enables you to concentrate on making the thick end bend first. It's all great fun!

# 13. Aerosol SprayPainting

I decided to try and finish my present model of the Victorian battleship HMS Camperdown (1885) using only acrylic car aerosols rather than my airbrush. The main reason for this is that I hate cleaning out airbrushes. The trouble with aerosols is that they lack the control built in to a good airbrush. They do tend to be either ON or OFF although some do allow a measure of control to the amount being sprayed. Aerosols are ideal of course for spraying big items such as hulls but I doubted their ability to cope with small items, which are typical of my kind of modelmaking.

However, so far, and the model is 90% complete, I have not had to use my airbrush. I have found the secret is in the speed of traverse of the aerosol, which is the only way to reduce the amount of paint hitting small objects. These are usually fixed to a strip of wood or anything convenient come to that, with double-sided sticky tape. I then hold the

**Fig 1. small object prepared for aerosol spray painting fixed to stick using double-sided sticky tape.**

**Fig 2. spraying is best carried out using swift passes to reduce the paint deposited during the pass.**

paint aerosol about 6in from it and spray using a "flicking" motion across the object. This can be repeated if necessary as one of the beauties of spraying is that you can spray wet on wet, which you certainly cannot with brushwork! There are two points to consider here. One is how you prepare the jobs, say a line of small objects for spraying. If you position them as shown in **Fig.1** then all surfaces can be sprayed in two passes. If the spray is directed down at 45 deg the top and one side will be covered followed by the same technique on the other side thus covering all surfaces. The 45 deg angle is arbitrary - a flatter angle will reduce top coverage as the top will get two doses anyway. The other way is to use three passes concentrating on each side and then the top. Speed of traverse is all-important to avoid over coverage. It is a technique that has to be learned. Aerosols left to their own devices will certainly overwhelm small items. **Fig.2** shows the completion of one pass.

The other point relates to how you stick the objects down. If you merely plonk them down onto the double-sided tape you do tend to get a fillet of paint forming at the junction of tape and part. This may be of no consequence especially if you remember the gospel according to King and keep paint application to a minimum to avoid swamping detail. In any case after removal from the tape, with the paint film fully hard, this fillet can be removed. Try sticking a strip of very fine abrasive paper to a 1in wide strip of wood making a "file" highly suitable for such jobs.

The sophisticated way is to stick a piece of masking tape to the base of the object before shoving it onto the double-sided tape. This piece of masking tape must be clear of the edges of course. You then have the base of the part clear of its support and therefore no fillet to worry about! If you also remember to brush off immediately before you spray to remove any dust you will not need to rub down either. I never have to rub down; only occasionally a scalpel is called for to remove

**Above: Authors model of Bouvet was aerosol spray painted - shown here during construction.**

the odd burr or lump that gets stuck in the paint film. Life just ain't perfect! Some items can be supported on pieces of wire, cocktail sticks or whatever, which nicely eliminates the need for double-sided tape but do remember to de-dust immediately before blasting on the paint.

One other important point is how you look after your aerosol. I always check that the spray nozzle is clear. Inverting the can and spraying the nozzle clear is recommended but also make sure there is not a paint build-up around the spray exit. Some cans show this phenomenon. If this paint is not removed it can splatter back onto the surface being sprayed. Remove it whilst still wet with a tissue and keep checking on its further build-up.

As always attention to seemingly insignificant detail is all-important in attaining, or trying to attain, perfection.

Use of water bound acrylics has many advantages over the older paints and enamels. They do not "skin" in the can, which was always the bugbear of the latter. They are quickly and easily mixed in a matter of

seconds again unlike oil bound materials. The range of colours now obtainable is great and you can get a colour match without much trouble. They are water-soluble until they have cured when only their dedicated thinners will have any effect on them. This means that brushes can be washed out in water unless any paint on them has started to cure. This may occur to paint on the bristles near the brush ferrule if you have been painting for a long time. To avoid this, wash out your brushes from time to time being careful to remove paint from this area of the bristles.

Although these paints now spray very well indeed (some makes did not at one time!) I find they do not brush well especially if the temperature is high as they tend to cure too fast. You just cannot "work" them like enamels as they start to cure, which completely messes up the finish. My technique is to flow the paint on with a minimum of brushing and never go back over a pre-painted area even if it appears to be still wet. If you do you will start to pick up semi-cured paint particles, which can be very vexing!

# 14. Cowl Ventilators

I had a letter from my friend Paul Freshney asking how you make cowl ventilators - the kind fitted to steamers? Those of us who make models of Victorian ships are always faced with this problem as most ships of this era sported forests of them. They disappeared of course with the advent of forced ventilation so modellers of later twentieth century ships do not have this problem.

Shipping line models of the early part of the twentieth century usually had silver plated cowl ventilators. This rather peculiar practice of plating various parts of these expensive models backfired as after a time the silver plated components turned streaky black - the tarnished silver. Unlike gold, silver does tarnish quite easily especially in foggy weather. As far as I can ascertain the cowl vents for these models were made by copper plating solid pre-cast lead cores. This was done by using electrolysis to plate to such a thickness as

**Fig 1. Punch and die used to produce copper ventilators.**

**Fig 2. Authors model of HMS Magnificent which features a large number of ventilators.**

to be self-sustaining after the lead had been melted out. Silver plating afterwards would be no problem.

The way I tackled making these cowl vents was to produce the copper cowl by deep forming and attaching this to a copper or brass tube. **Fig.1** shows a punch and die that was used to produce some of the cowls shown in **Fig.2**, which is my model of HMS Magnificent. The easiest way is to put the die into the three-jaw chuck of the lathe and the punch into the tailstock. The lathe can then be used as a press. Hold the annealed copper sheet between punch and die using the tailstock to drive the punch and metal into the die. Stop immediately an increase in resistance is felt and re-anneal the sheet. This is done by heating to red heat and, for convenience, quenching in cold water. Continue the process until the cowl is completely formed. If you hurry the process or inadequately anneal the

cowl will fracture and you will have to start from scratch again. This is the difficult part. The column is relatively easy. The top end needs to be machined or filed to fit the cowl remembering its position relative to the column. Some Victorian cowls protruded over the back of the column. This shape was very typical of the period.

I soft solder the cowl to the column and fill with Isopon to produce a smooth junction between the two components. Before finally cleaning up the shape put the hole in the cowl to match the hole in the column. I use dental burrs for this job.

This is the best method but it requires a certain degree of mechanical expertise and a large amount of patience to achieve a good result. The other problems are, you really need a hearth, a fairly large gas torch (copper conducts heat away at a phenomenal rate) and someone to pay the gas bill. You can do

**Fig 3. A selection of the raw pressings produced by the tool shown in Fig 1.**

without the lathe acting as a press and just hold the punch over the die but the lathe does ensure the punch lines up with the die and eliminates one source of trouble.

When I retired from the Technical College those facilities vanished so I looked for another practicable method. The solution was to substitute plastic (ABS) for copper sheet. The only heat you then require is to form the cowl. I use boiling water but this has the obvious danger of scalding unless really adequate protection of the hands is undertaken. I put the die and a strip of plastic in the boiling or near boiling, water and push down on the punch really hard. Polystyrene sheet can be used instead of ABS and it certainly requires less heat and less force than the latter but its life is more problematic. Also Isopon does not adhere very well to polystyrene sheet although Milliput is an effective substitute.

However, nothing can be done without the tooling - punch and die. As can be seen from **Fig.3** it is the punch, the male member, that controls the size and shape of the product.

The interior diameter of the cowl will be the same size as the punch. The die, in essence, is merely a hole with the top edge slightly radiused to aid the flow of material as the punch enters. The size of the hole will be the diameter of the punch plus two thickness of material plus say another 0.005in for clearance. Try using 0.015in thick material as a start, which should give good results on cowls up to 1in diameter. Very small cowls will need thinner material and vice versa. Remember the final thickness of the cowl will be less than the initial sheet thickness due to the stretching taking place during the forming operation. It can be fun to put a grid of lines onto the sheet before forming with a felt pen and examine how the sheet distorts during the forming process.

The shape of the punch in Fig.1 could have been improved by making a bigger flange. This would flatten out the sheet around the "dimple" and reduce or eliminate the "cockles" that occur as a result of the material being dragged into the die. This effect can be seen in Fig.3. The flange on the die also acts as

**Above: Very prominent ventilators such as these on Empress of India do require carefully thought out tooling if they are to end up identical.**

a stop of course and a gauge of how deep the forming has progressed. Of course a more sophisticated tool could have a plate fixed above the die to stop the material cockling in the first place but as all this material is cut off anyway this is not absolutely necessary. Fig.3 shows a collection of cowl mouldings. The left hand copper one has failed - note the crack at its base. The grey ones are ABS and the completed white ones are styrene. The markings on the copper are due to the annealing process.

I have also dreamed up another way of making cowl vents but have never put it into practice. It is to, in effect, bisect the ventilator vertically and make press tools for the right and left hand halves, joining these together afterwards of course. This would work I am sure but the tool making involved is

frightening. For a large number of the same size it might be contemplated however. Sometimes very small, and I mean very small, vents are required for such things as ship's boats. I have made these from one sixteenth diameter aluminium rod or the shank of a long rivet with the end bent at right angles with the interior of the bell hacked out with a dental burr. Alternatively a piece of ABS tube can be used with the cowl itself carved from a lump of attached Isopon or Milliput. Remember we are talking about very small vents.

Finally a lot of vents have some furniture attached: handles for turning them, crossed members reinforcing the opening, even chain driven wheels to turn the tops of tall ones. The interiors were often painted bright red, which can add a nice touch of colour to a model.

# 15. Main Armament

With warship models the main armament always catches the eye as it is the raison d'être for the ship's existence in the first place. So its execution must be as good as possible. Making model gun barrels appears to be as difficult as making the real thing. The guns on battleships usually took longer to build than the rest of the ship and were often the limiting factor when it came to delivery time. By the nature of things large, gun barrels usually consist of a number of tapered sections fitted together. There are several ways of tackling the problem. Perhaps the easiest is to find, if you can a number of interlocking tubes of the correct sizes and join them together with adhesive or solder. This will certainly give you the "stepped" appearance of a large gun barrel and was the way large barrels were actually made in practice. Although in full size practice the parts were shrunk together using an interference fit between the "hoops" and a great deal of heat to actually do the deed.

The Beardmore, Parkehead gun factory had a 90ft deep oil bath sunk into the ground filled with 126 tons of oil for this work. Above it was a 130 ton Goliath crane with a clear lift of 100ft. Talk about big boy's toys!

Coming back to the model world barrels made from interlocking tubes lack the essential gun barrel taper. The result is that it all looks a bit amateurish. The fact is that gun barrel taper is essential if the weapon is to look realistic.

The best way is to use a lathe if you have one of course. The degree of difficulty really depends on the length/diameter ratio. Guns with low ratios can be turned between centres as they are stiff enough to withstand the stress of taper turning. The great advantage of turning between centres is that the work can be removed and replaced any number of times without losing concentricity. This is important, as each tapered section really needs to be turned on all the barrels in the batch at the same lathe setting.

Let me explain: setting angles on the lathe top slide accurately is not really possible; it always becomes a matter of trial and error. Setting accurate angles on many machines is difficult and is one cross, as a machinist that you have to bear. It can be done by using a master taper and a dial test indicator (a "clock" as we of the fraternity call it) but for most ship modellers that is a bit advanced.

With slender gun barrels (high length/diameter ratios) treating the whole length of the barrel becomes difficult, as it is not stiff

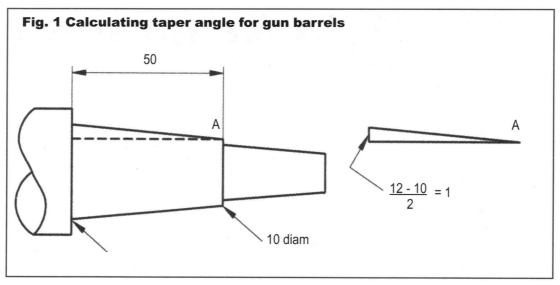

**Fig. 1 Calculating taper angle for gun barrels**

enough to resist the turning forces. In this case hold the job between the three-jaw chuck and tailstock. If you face and bore the muzzle first, the reversed drill in a drill chuck held in the tailstock will give much wanted support whilst turning. If you also mark the chuck end at, say jaw no.1 re-chucking at the same position should retain reasonable concentricity. Always, but always, do not forget to lubricate the muzzle bore and drill at the tailstock end otherwise you may end up with the drill welded in the bore or, worse still, sheared off. When turning tapers I always turn the major diameter parallel first. After getting the taper setting correct (by trial and error remember) all you need to do is to turn the whole length of your parallel part tapered and if the angle is correct the job will be done i.e. the small end of the taper will be to size.

We talk about size but what size? Apart from the bore we usually have no definite dimension. The first step is to make a drawing and work out the angles. You will find four or possibly six or more drawings of your barrel on the plan drawings. Unfortunately every drawing will be slightly different. You have to select one as a sample and mark it for future reference. Put all length dimensions and major and minor diameters on your drawing. From the major and minor diameters of a given taper you can use trigonometry to work out the angle A which you need to be able to set the top slide of your lathe. **Fig.1**. In trig terms $\tan A = \text{opp}/\text{adj} = 1/50 = 0.02$. From trig tables (or your calculator) $A = 1.15\text{deg}$.

If number crunching is not your thing and you have no "wunderkind" in your family an alternative way to get at this angle is to draw the above triangle out, say 10x size or even larger and measure the required angle with a protractor. This should be close enough as you usually have to modify the set angle slightly anyway to allow for the "spring" in the system. Care should be taken with the shape of the muzzle; particularly the exaggerated muzzle swell needed for weapons made of cast iron. The shape at the muzzle can be quite subtle and must be copied closely to truly replicate the barrel. Incidentally the large muzzle swell was necessary, as cast iron is not very strong in tension and hence in resisting the bursting pressures exerted by the charge. At every point along the barrel the portion of the barrel in front of the shot is supporting the part behind the shot which is being subject to the bursting force. At the muzzle this no longer applies so extra strength is needed to

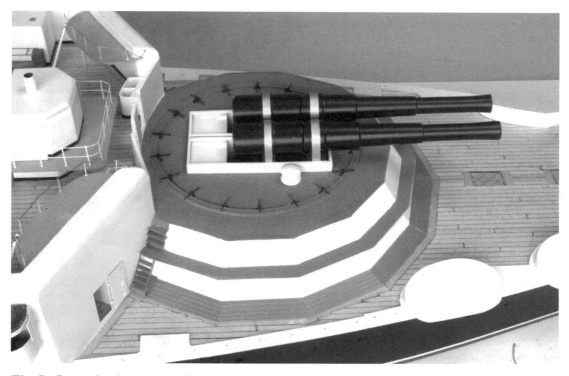

**Fig 2. Guns in the partially completed barbette of HMS Camperdown. Note the muzzle swell.**

avoid it breaking. It won't peel back like a banana as cast iron has no ductility to speak of – it will just shatter probably giving everyone standing near a bit.

In the absence of a lathe, interlocking tubes, etc the power drill clamped (carefully) in a vice or stand with files, etc can be used. Great feats have been achieved with this method and indeed it may be the only way to produce "turned" parts if other facilities are denied to you but accuracy and repeatability will undoubtedly suffer.

Casting gun barrels (non-working of course)

using a wood or metal pattern and silicon rubber moulds is a possibility particularly if large numbers are required. At least all should be identical whereas separately turned ones may not be! Incidentally if you do get slight errors showing up simply select pairs that match. Gun barrels at the opposite end of a ship cannot be easily compared whereas in close proximity they can!

**Fig.2** shows the partially completed barbette and guns from my model of HMS Camperdown. It shows perfectly the muzzle swell on an 1890's steel gun barrel.

# 16. Fittings

## Part 1

Scratch building continually throws up problems that have to be solved. Sometimes the problem is how to make something not attempted before but often it is merely an improvement on something already achieved. Making eyebolts probably comes in the later category. I usually have to make a fair number for one of my models for belaying lines to, etc. I have spent some time experimenting to try and improve the result and to speed up what can be a boring process.

This is the sequence I have worked out. You need a pair of round-nosed pliers with points small enough for the job, a pair of sharp cutters and a pair of pointed pliers with serrated jaws.

Start by using the round-nosed pliers to produce **Fig.1**. Note the "straight" part of the curve "X" which you do not want, so using the cutters clip off at point A. Using the

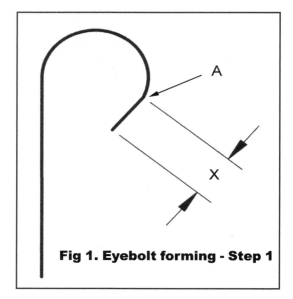

**Fig 1. Eyebolt forming - Step 1**

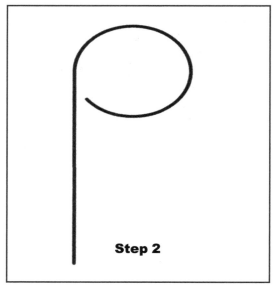

**Step 2**

round-nosed pliers continue to pull the curve round until the job looks as at **Fig.2**. Note with the flat part "X" removed this is now possible. Try and close the loop completely. The serrated pliers may help here. The serrations will grip the wire and enable you to "coax" the loop closed. Finally pull the loop to the left to complete the job as in **Fig.3**.

With a bit of practice you can produce identical eyebolts quite quickly and easily. When using the cutters note if they produce a sharp cut on one side and a sloping cut on the other. If so use the sharp side to trim off part "X". One of the things that I always try to remove, as far as possible, is the need for really accurate work, which takes time and skill. If there is an easier way around the problem I try to find it. Whilst attempting to fit bollards to my model I thought a discussion of ways and means would show what I mean. For instance, I always like a positive location. **Fig.4** shows a bollard held in tweezers just over where it is to finally sit. You will note that the unit consists of two identical brass turnings produced with a fixing spigot attached to an ABS base plate. You will also notice the mating holes pre-drilled into the deck edges.

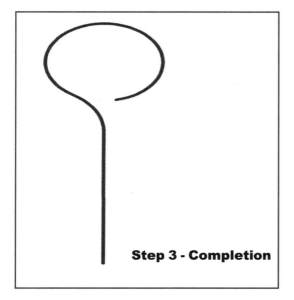

**Step 3 - Completion**

There appears to be at least four ways of fixing the bollards:

1. Cut off the two spigots leaving a flat base and simply glue the bollards down. OK but not very strong and no positive location of the part.

2. Mark out carefully and drill two fitted holes for the spigots. This requires skill both in marking out and drilling not to mention time.

3. Before assembling the bollard unit use its base as a template for drilling the deck fitting holes. The problem here is holding the template in the right place. Easy in theory but difficult in practice.

4. Mark out and drill two oversize holes, partially fill with Isopon or Milliput, and seat the bollards in the correct relationship with the deck edge. Just leave to set. This would be my favourite method as it is so much easier to do and requires no real accuracy. Make sure there is no burr on the holes to prevent the bollards sitting down properly or too much filler for the same reason.

The above reminds one that most problems have more than one solution so do not necessarily take the first solution that pops into your brain. Often there is a better way. By better I mean faster, more accurate or easier to carry out. Model making, especially at the higher levels of scratch building, requires much time and skill and it behoves you to try and simplify anything that can be simplified. There are always the jobs that will try your skill(s) to the utmost. Spend your efforts on those.

Lastly in this Column a bit more about the evils of dust. Here he goes again about dust, his favourite topic seemingly, I hear you say. Well I make no apologies for mentioning this subject again, as most modellers simply are not aware of the problem it causes.

I have been photographing detail on my latest model in view of doing a write-up for the further delectation of the readers of this magazine. Editor permitting, of course! This has been done using a digital camera with a macro lens and the results examined at about

**Fig 4. Bollards just prior to permanently fixing into position.**

A4 size on the computer screen. The subject when photographed appeared perfectly dust free but the computer showed otherwise. Unless a dusting brush had been carefully applied beforehand the results were useless. The black areas in particular showed how much dust had adhered to the surface. If the area had been sprayed and not merely photographed this dust would have been incorporated into the paint film, which would require a rub down as a consequence. All this just emphasises the need to use a clean brush before either painting or photographing unless, of course, rubbing down is your thing! An interesting case did occur when we were

photographing the Admiral's walk way round the stern of one of my Victorian battleships. The image was on the screen at about A4 size, really an enormous magnification from the 35mm original. We noticed a ghostly object seemingly crouching behind the ornate cast iron railings surrounding the Admiral's walk at the stern. Whatever it was it should not have been there but we could not identify it. On looking at the model we discovered it to be a Perspex porthole slug. On further inspection we discovered an empty port from whence it had obviously come but how it got to where we found it mystifies me. Perhaps I have a Rumpel Stiltskin in my shipyard.

## CHAPTER 16

**Above: HMS Camperdown finished bollards etc. can be seen fitted into their final locations.**

# 17. Developing Compound Angled Shapes

When I started this series of columns I asked for subjects to write about, problems that needed solving. One such question that Geoff Spencer came up with was developing the shape of the multiple facets of a Type 22 frigate's bridge. This was really an exercise in technical drawing and I undertook to work out the shapes for Geoff, which in itself

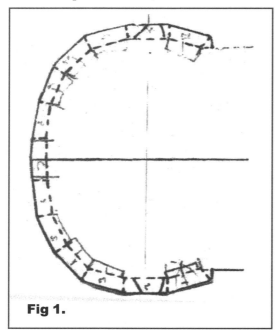

**Fig 1.**

would provide material for this column. To start with you need ACCURATE drawings of the plan shape and side elevation or a section through the bridge to show the true lengths and angles. It is quite useless to try and develop shapes from inaccurate sketches. These sketches must be cleaned up. It is necessary to try and get into the mind of the Naval architect who originally designed the bridge. It is a fair bet that all the segments of the bridge would be of the same length unless there is an obvious reason for a difference. You will find these lengths on the drawing (sketch) will not be quite the same and these differences must be worked out. This can be done using a pencil, rule, straight edge and protractor and fiddling around until some sort of sense and order has been established as close as possible to the original sketch. This may be called the manual, first principle, way of working. The original information with which I started is shown in **Fig.1.**

However, we found the best way was to scan the sketch into the computer and using a drawing programme (CAD), to put some accuracy into the deal. This is largely a subjective process based on your assessment of what the shape should be. The cleaned up

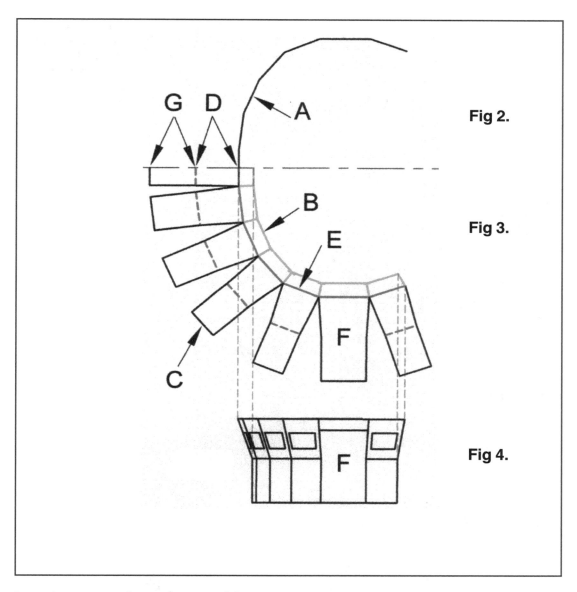

Fig 2.

Fig 3.

Fig 4.

image is constructed over the scan of the sketch. The sketch can then be erased to leave your accurately reconstructed shape (line A). **Fig.2**. If the shape is symmetrical only half needs to be drawn as the computer can mirror this half to give you the complete deal. **Fig.2** shows this shape, which is now ready for adding the developed shapes, which will make up the actual sides of the bridge. Firstly a line must be drawn round the inside of the

plan shape to indicate the position of the vertical part of the sides (line B). This is shown in **Fig.3**. (Please note on Fig.3 there should be a horizontal line on panel F near the top as in **Fig.4**. Above this line is an extension of the sloping part of the sides whereas the rest of panel F is set in vertically and houses the water tight door). The intersection of these lines gives you the width of the vertical part of the sides i.e. C. Think about it! These

**Left: The bridge of HMS Belfast incorporated extensive use of etched brass.**

lines must be at right angles to the related line marked E i.e. the top edge of the side.

The true length of the sloping part of the walls can only be taken from the side elevation (sheer) or a section through the bridge if available. **Fig.4**. The dashed lines show the correlation between **Fig.3** and **Fig.4**.

The two panels marked F have a standard watertight door set into them and the surface has therefore to be vertical. This requires tapered "gussets" to fill in the space between the vertical and the "tumblehome" of the "window" slope of the upper part of the sides. These two panels port and starboard therefore are different from the rest of the side panels.

The solving of this sort of problem really requires a knowledge of engineering drawing, of projection and an understanding of the meaning of the true length of lines. Many lines shown on normal orthogonal three-view drawings are foreshortened because they do not lie in the planes of the drawing. In simple terms they are not parallel to the paper on which the view is drawn. To enable true scale developments to be drawn you must be able to determine what is the true length of any given line however it is drawn. In the case described you need **Fig.4** (which is an elevation of the port side of the bridge) to enable the length of the sloping part of the side to be measured (D). Note G and D are true line lengths.

As an etching job the construction is simple. All you need is a complete etching although only half is shown is **Fig.3**. I would half-etch all the folding lines (shown in green) enabling the vertical sides to be folded down from the deck head (i.e. the roof) and the sides kinked to accommodate the inward sloping window panels. This method has the advantage of keeping all the parts together (i.e. no joints). The base could be another etching following the interior red line. The whole is then soldered up. Otherwise the top and bottom could be a thicker piece of plastic or wood with the vertical parts possibly made of Plasticard glued into position. You would need to accurately position the top and bottom both in plan position and distance to act as a foundation before attempting to glue the sides. If the top were of any thickness it would need to be chamfered to accommodate the aforesaid sloping panels. How you build the bridge largely depends on whether you are interested in the interior. The whole thing could be solid with only the interior removed behind the windows. It is really a case of paying the money and taking your choice! Anyway, thanks Geoff for an interesting problem.

# 18. Shrouds and Ratlines

I dedicated my first book "Advanced Ship Modelling" (Special Interest Model Books) to all those who strive for perfection knowing they will never achieve it, but struggle on just the same! I suppose that about sums up my own philosophy – I continually strive for perfection, for better, faster, simpler and more perfect ways of doing things. I think most model makers concentrate on the workshop scene, the practical, and the physical part of the action. Whereas I think more medals are probably won at half past two in the morning when the solution to the problem decides to make its presence known! Fanciful? I think not.

Scratch building is full of problems and no amount of previous experience eliminates all of them and in any case I find I have forgotten how I did it last time anyhow!

All this has been brought on by having to rig shrouds and ratlines on my model of HMS Camperdown. I thought it would make a good Column to analyse this particular problem and see how I think it should be tackled.

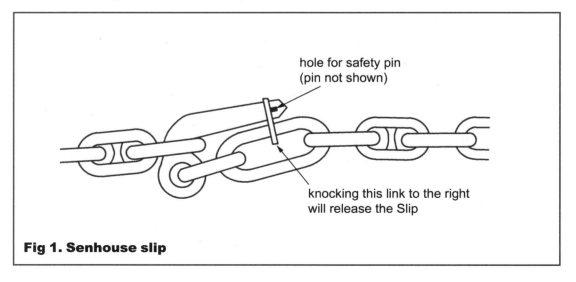

hole for safety pin
(pin not shown)

knocking this link to the right
will release the Slip

**Fig 1. Senhouse slip**

**Fig 2. Shrouds and ratlines on HMS Belfast.**

As I see it there are three stages to the job. How are you going to do it, if you like?
1. The Method.
2. The materials and tools and selection of the same.
3. Actually doing the job.
You need to study your drawings and particularly any detail photos of what was done on the ship itself. Gone are the two blocks set above the chains rigged with a connecting rope to adjust the set of each individual shroud. (Chain – outboard securing place for rigging, shrouds, etc). Victorian warships used bottle screws (right and left-

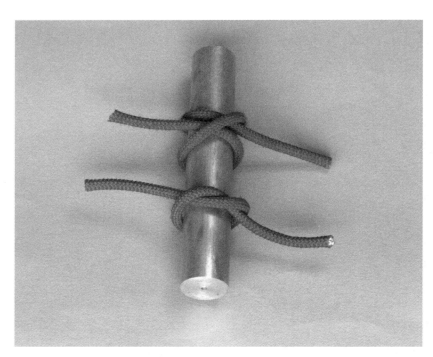

**Fig 3. Clove hitch and plain half hitch.**

hand threads) to tighten the shroud lines and possibly a Senhouse slip **Fig.1** as well. Luckily for the model maker all this gear was usually covered with a canvas sleeve, tarred or painted thus relieving him of making all this detail. **Fig.2** shows the completed shrouds and ratlines. Note the way both ends of each shroud are belayed off through the eyes fitted to the mast barrel and the top of the bulwark. Note the latter were usually attached to a strap that distributed the load. In my case these straps were merely added on for verisimilitude and were not functional. With the three shrouds fitted and correctly tensioned the ratlines can be tied on. However, have you used the correct sized thread for the shrouds?

A great deal of work is required tying off the ratlines so do not proceed until you are sure the thread size and the material chosen is right. Compare what you have done with any photos you have, ask a knowledgeable friend, run a Mori pole if necessary but do not continue until you are satisfied the job is correct. Of course if you are scratch building

the decision is yours but even when kit building the manufacturers choice of thread may be wrong. Probably things have improved of late but in the past threads supplied in some kits have been questionable as to their suitability. If necessary other threads can be substituted of course and certainly should be if you have any doubts on that score. Do not spoil the ship for a happorth of tar! The question of thread and wire (rod) sizes on a model do cause trouble because there is not an infinite choice. Wire, for instance, are only made in specific gauges. When in doubt always go for the thinner size if faced with a choice. Nothing looks worse than oversize detail on a model. With the thinner choice one can always slap on an extra coat of paint but saddled with oversize detail little can be done. This point cannot really be over-emphasised whether you are a beginner to the game or have achieved the "sear and yellow" like wot I have.

If, after thought, everything is satisfactory tying on the ratlines is the next operation. The same remarks regarding selection of material apply here. Tying off "n" ratlines only to find that they look too thick or thin can try the calmest soul! As everyone knows the correct knots to use are clove hitches on intermediate shrouds but these are not used on the outside lines. In full sized practice the ratlines have an eye worked in each end and these are lashed to the outermost shrouds. So now you know. Unless the model is to a large scale full-sized practice is obviously not possible. Clove hitches, **Fig.3**, may still be possible and I tried these but at the scale I was working they looked too bulky. I experimented with various knots but eventually settled on plain half hitches, Fig.3, on all the shroud lines including the outside ones. When finally adjusted a touch of runny cyano applied with a syringe sealed them. Sealing this way enables very close cropping of the excess ends as the cyano produces a rigid thread for cutting unlike the normal unglued, limp end that tends to whisker. If left over-long the ends are known in the trade as Irish pennants I believe.

Two points require care. Do not over-tighten the ratlines as they tend to "waist" the shrouds - which looks bad. Also make sure the thread chosen ties well whatever the material is. For instance some mercerised cotton threads are rather stiff and do not lend themselves to bending around the shrouds. This "minor" point takes on an important role if each ratline covers say, six shrouds — the total number of knots to tie becomes astronomic. To achieve a consistent appearance the method of tying off needs to be maintained. I found that with only three shrouds to deal with tying the central shroud off first and then always the left hand one followed by the right. I found bringing the loose end from right to left round behind the vertical shroud and then OVER the horizontal piece and then up to form the half hitch worked well but any consistent operation would do.

Are there any other ways of making shrouds and ratlines? This is a question one should always ask. Amati make a "Loom a Line" which comprise an adjustable frame on which a set of shrouds can be built up. Whether you would prefer to use this or rely on making up the shrouds in situ is your choice. For very small sets of shrouds etching could be used but again you must decide if an etched shroud set would be acceptable. A close friend of mine who is a superb model maker of the diorama school has his double blocks above the chain etched.

# 19. Ship's Boats Open Boats

A plethora of ship's boats are required for any large ship being modelled. Victorian battleships always had a large number ready for any off-shore work likely to be required during the days of Empire with the RN having to maintain several large fleets around the world to keep the Pax Britannica.

I have long since decided that a suite of ship's boats needs to be treated as a separate job, as making up to sixteen little models in their own right is a big enough effort to exclude everything else. There are, of course, several ways of tackling this problem. To start with they can be separated into two classes: open boats like whalers, gigs, etc. and closed boats such as torpedo vessels and Admiral's barges. The open boats I used to carve from wood split along the vertical centreline with a plywood keel inserted. I found the main problem was making them thin enough to avoid them looking a trifle clumsy. To avoid this I then made them from moulded polystyrene sheet. These moulded hulls can be made using only a shaped male plug with a simple hole as the female die. The only problem with this is that the concave shape at the deadwood on square-sterned boats cannot be made unless a shaped female form is also used. You can, however, ignore this

concave shape by moulding the bottom as shown in **Fig.1** and filling in the concave space between the hull underside and the keel or deadwood with a filler – either Milliput or polyester paste. You need to use the former on mouldings made from styrene as polyester paste does not readily stick to styrene, as it does to ABS sheet, which is what I now use to make boat mouldings. A point to remember is that with square-sterned boats it is best to ignore the flat transom and mould an extended round stern, which is easier to mould. A separate transom can be fitted before cutting off the extended round portion. In this way a clean sharp-cornered stern is obtained. Trying to mould in a flat stern always results in a "sucked sweet" appearance and you get people murmuring in their beards that this bloke does not know his job. Always a situation best avoided – murmuring in beards that is.

The other problem is thinning of the moulding at the maximum stress points such as the fore foot and at both ends of the whalers. This can be easily seen if the moulding is held up to the light. Using thicker sheet material is one cure, slightly altering the shape of the male plug at this point is another if this can be tolerated visually. In any case

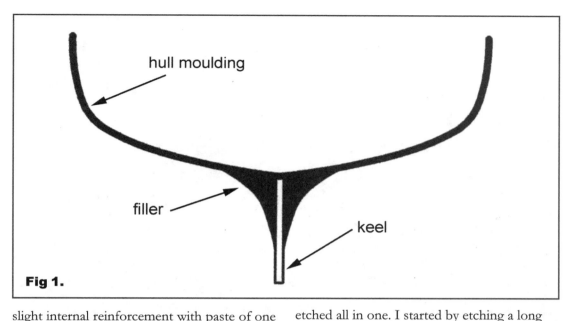

hull moulding

filler

keel

**Fig 1.**

slight internal reinforcement with paste of one kind or another is a good idea but limit the amount used as it may interfere with the subsequent fitting of footboards, etc.
Fitting Out. With the shell of the boat prepared fitting out is the next step. With the wooden types I usually fit an inwale all round the inner margins of the boat and "spring-in" the timbers (ribs) made from wood or plastic strips. A certain amount of experimenting is required to get the size and consistency of the rib strips right to enable the strips to spring in and retain themselves. Fitting the strips as a long boring job as each one is a different length. A couple of days of this sort of work finds me contemplating the monastic life.
It occurred to me that the timbers could be

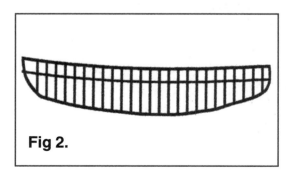

**Fig 2.**

etched all in one. I started by etching a long central spine with the ribs sprouting from it at right angles like a fish bone. This was "dressed" into the boat shell with the ends of the ribs trimmed off to fit under the inwale. The etching needs to be carefully annealed before it is soft enough to dress and stay put in the moulding. Trying to fit an unannealed etching is impossible – try it.
Being quick of thought it took me some time to realise I was definitely barking up the wrong tree and tackling the job the wrong way round. You did not want the ribs attached to aforesaid spine but to the inwale. This is shown in Fig.2, which is a rib etching for a 27ft whaler. You need to cut paper patterns to determine roughly the shape of the inwale. Sometimes it can be a straight line but it usually requires to be curved to a greater or lesser degree to ensure a fit. The lower ends of the ribs will end up under the footboards, which will hide any mess. This had the making of a cunning plan – which it is. The sharp ones amongst my readers will note that the lower ends of the ribs are joined together and as such will not fit into the moulding. The reason for this is to firstly strengthen the etching itself but this line needs

**Whaler from HMS Queen Elizabeth.**

to be cut and any excess snipped out on assembly. Secondly, the remnants of this piece also provide extra gluing area for fixing. The "horizontal" mid member represents the "shelf" which provides a support for the thwarts. With sharply curved boats (in the transverse plane) such as gigs excess length may have to be removed from this member to get a fit. The shelf actually sits on the ribs and is not coincident as it is with an etching but you cannot have everything in this life. At a small scale this is not noticeable and if it is another strip could be glued on.

Actually I have toyed with the idea of making an etching, which includes all the thwarts and the shelf, but it is very difficult to get a fit even if you make a cardboard template first. I have therefore reverted to a ribs/shelf etching and fitting the thwarts as separate wood details instead.

Other etched parts that can be made are the rudder and oars although other methods and materials can be easily substituted. Remember footboards are usually made from a number of planks and these can be represented as either half-etching or with actual spaces between the planks but you need some cross-linking to avoid a handful of separate bits to fit in somehow! For larger boats the double knees usually seen at each end of the thwarts can also be added as etchings. These are a difficult shape to make using orthodox methods.

I had intended to deal with closed boats but space has vanished – perhaps another Column.

# 20. Ship's Boats - Closed Boats

In my last Column I had hoped to discuss both open and closed boats but in the event I only managed to talk about open boats so in this one we are on to closed boats i.e. those with a deck and superstructure. In some ways this type is easier to model, although often looking more complicated than the open type, as usually no shell and hence no moulding plug and die is required; the hull being a carving. In some cases the stern area may need to be hollowed out to form the stern sheets (area for passenger accommodation). If carving out this space

from the solid is a problem the boat could be made in the same way as a moulded open boat and the rest of the hull filled in. How you do this will largely depend on its actual size.

If the boat is to be carved I have found that starting off correctly saves endless trouble later. For instance, I always start with an accurate block of wood large enough to completely encompass the final hull. Make sure it is an accurate prism although large amounts will be carved away eventually. The reason for this is twofold. Firstly I cut a

**Fig 1. 42ft launch fitted to the authors model of HMS Camperdown.**

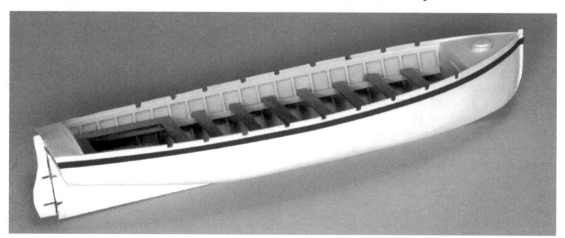

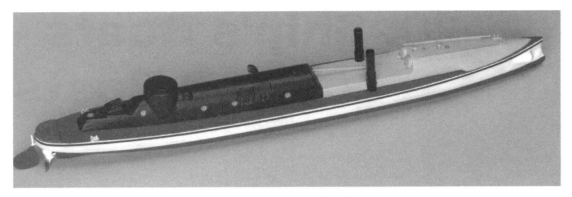

**Fig 2. This torpedo boat also fitted to HMS Camperdown.**

groove along its base and at least the bow (it may also need one at the stern) for the keel, stem post, etc. I also cut transverse slots in the base for the crutches. I usually use my miniature circular saw for these slots. One advantage of a "solid" boat is that instead of having to cut the crutches to fit the hull shape they can be solid and just slotted into the hull. The outside can then be trimmed to shape. This eliminates the problem of fixing the crutches firmly, always difficult with open boats. It is relatively easy to cut these transverse slots when the hull is still a geometrically accurate block. However, you do need to get them in the right place especially if they are to sit on a set of skid beams. Torpedo boats often have four or five supports along their length and these need to fit accurately onto their respective supports if tears at a later date are to be avoided. These remarks really refer to late Victorian battleships but the principle is universal. These boats usually have a rubbing strake near or at the top edge of the hull. If the hull size is appropriate this can be added after painting with a Letraset strip or possibly a car body stripe. Experience has taught me NOT to stretch this tape on application as it will then, all on its own without permission, shrink back to the length it wants to be leaving a gap at one end or the other. Nasty! To stop it coming unstuck at the ends I also apply a dab of extra adhesive such as cyano to fix the

ends. Needless to say this tape really needs to be rubbed down firmly after you have got it on correctly. Examine it from all quarters to make sure you have a fair run before you do this of course. The use of tape enables a suitable coloured strip to be chosen and gives a clean piece of detailing.

Some of these boats, in fact most of them, will have engines and hence propellers which can be a problem owing to their small size. If you are into etching these can be etched. In my book "Advanced Ship Modelling" I show a method of producing small propellers from wire, which sounds daft but can look quite well in practice.

As ship's boats form an important part of the visual scene when the model is exhibited great care should be lavished on them. You do see on some large models the boats treated very casually, as something not very important and it always shows. Try and get as much detail into them as possible. If you are using etching do not forget such things as handrails, rudders, hatches, steering wheels, the aforesaid propellers and anything else that can be etched. So often such ancillary items get forgotten as dealing with the parent vessel becomes the most important thing.

When fitting any ship's boats particularly those stowed on crutches make sure the boat sits upright (truly perpendicular), which usually means that the lower edge of the crutches has to be slightly angled to take into account the

## CHAPTER 20

**Fig 3. Complete suite of boats fitted to HMS Camperdoen.**

deck (or beam) camber. Always allow extra material for this to make sure the boat is installed on the side it was designed to fit! It is easy in the excitement of finally getting something put together to make a mistake. Well I have! Care also needs to be taken to get the boat "level" fore and aft. This is controlled by the height of the crutches. Another point to watch is that all crutches are "sitting down" with no air space under any of them. By and large I find fitting the boats with their bows slightly higher than their sterns gives the best impression. Incidentally I always fit crutches to the boat and not the deck first. Some ships carrying large boat suites have some nested i.e. a 42ft launch may carry a smaller open boat inside it with yet another smaller one inside that one. In this case you can hope that somewhere you can find a cross section showing these internal crutches supporting the upper two boats. What you do need is to get the heights correct. In the absence of a cross section the sheer (side elevation) drawing may give the necessary information. Well you can hope! In some cases it would appear that some thwarts on

the lower boats have been temporarily removed.

Remember that boats not being used as sea boats and equipped with rudders mounted on pintles have these unshipped and laying in the stern sheets. Sea boats are those, usually one each side, already swung out ready for use and may have the rudders in place with the tiller arm lashed to prevent the rudder from swinging about. Larger powered vessels usually have permanently fixed rudders, which are wheel controlled, and cannot easily be unshipped.

For the newcomers to the hobby it is usual to display models starboard side on. Don't ask me why! Also all ship's boats should have their bows toward the bow of the parent vessel. All in all ship's boats are complicated, interesting additions to a model and should receive as much attention if not more than the rest of the model.

**Fig.1** is the 42ft launch and **Fig.2** is the torpedo boat made for my model of HMS Camperdown. **Fig.3** is more or less a complete suite of ship's boats for my HMS Magnificent all at a scale of 1:110.

# 21. The Bread and Butter Hull

## Part 1

When you see a fine model and then discover that all the detail work has been built onto a bought hull it all becomes a bit of an anticlimax. I always ask myself why? Surely building the hull gives you maximum return for minimum effort, or does it? Talking to modellers, which I do at every occasion possible, you often find that they wish that they had built the hull as at the final count, the hull does not come up to the standard they have set with the fitting out. There is also the problem of having to remove over-enthusiastic detailing on the purchased hull. This latter can be a real problem that also occurs on plastic kits.

One reason why some hulls are bought and not made is the lack of workshop facilities. Of the two main methods of hull building,

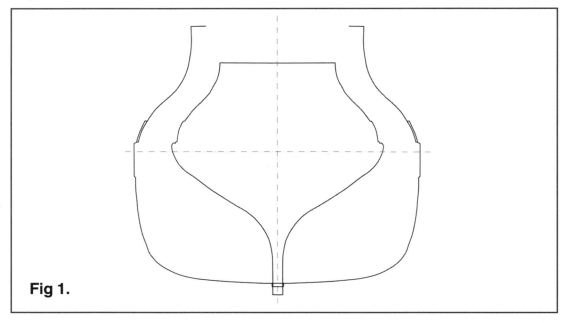

**Fig 1.**

**Fig 2. Using a hole saw to cut out the gun emplacements.**

plank on frame usually requires less facilities than my chosen method of carving the hull, which really does need a proper workshop with large vices. Another requirement may be that the distaff side of the family tolerates the inevitable mess that large scale carving produces.

When I look back to when I was about eleven I used to carve out hulls from solid lumps of pine. The tools I had were one indifferent saw, a wooden block plane, one 0.5in diameter wood drill and brace, and three chisels two of which the blades were about 2in long. They were rejects thrown out by my grandfather. To sharpen these tools I had a bit of a broken natural oilstone also retrieved as a discard. All this was a very long time ago and how I managed to make a boat hull with such poor facilities is now beyond me. These were all working boats and the method of hollowing out the inside was to drill a series of half inch holes with the aforementioned drill all round the hull leaving about a half inch thick wall. The interior was

hacked out with the longest of the three chisels - I must have been keen!

Nowadays I use the bread and butter system and bandsaw out the layers both inside and out. On the surface it's all very simple – you make all the layers and glue them together. Or is it? Long experience has taught me that in principle it is simple but there are a number of pitfalls that are very easy to fall into. You just cannot afford to make mistakes with wood as expensive as it is. My last model HMS Camperdown I built as a waterline model, which did raise a few eyebrows as my models are always of the full hull type. Waterline hulls save so much work - no propellers, drive shafts, A-frames, rudders and a lot of carving and painting is avoided. However, my new model, the French pre-dreadnought Bouvet is to be a full hull model and the bench in my workshop bears the scars. This hull is typical of the French and Russian ships of the time with a hull section like a truncated onion. Exaggerated tumblehome with complex concave curves; it

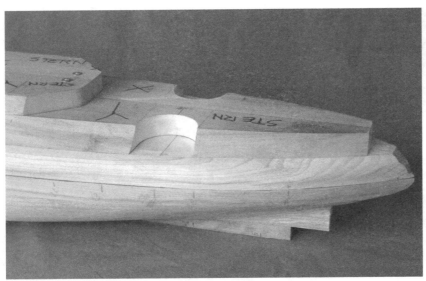

really is a carver's nightmare. **Fig.1** shows two sections through the hull. The outer shows a typical section about midships and the inner a section near the stern. They both show a complication not found in RN ships. I have used eight layers including the bottom. The thickness of the layers was chosen to facilitate the position of armoured belts and gun positions. One feature with these hulls is the necessary cut-outs to provide a horizontal bed for some of the gun turrets. Again this is a design feature not really found in the RN. Luckily the diameter of these cut-outs was 52mm (2in to the enlightened Brits!). It meant buying a 2in hole saw and mandrel to make a proper job of cutting out these emplacements. **Fig.2** shows the job being done. The hole cutter has a central drill for location but I was not sure that cutting only part of a hole would give a good enough finish so scrap pieces of wood were glued to the basic hull shape to ensure that a complete hole was cut. These cutouts were finished off and primed before the relevant lift was glued into the stack. This was easier to do at this stage rather than cleaning up after the stack was glued up. Glued in lines, between the layers and vertically through the keel provide useful and highly accurate datums when

shaping and fitting external detail. So the thickness of the layers is not arbitrary but requires care in selection.

Now comes the tricky bit. Although the French plans were quite comprehensive and in many ways more than adequately detailed they did not include a set of waterlines, which is essential if building bread and butter as you need them to cut out the layers. They gave a set of transverse sections (Fig.1 shows two of these) but did not show at what longitudinal position along the hull they were taken! However, further investigation (that means looking at the plans a bit longer) showed that more than the usual number of detailed cross-sections were drawn out and furthermore the longitudinal position of each was given and matched with the frame numbers found on the sheer and plan. Light now appeared at the end of the tunnel as a few hours work, coupled with a bit of guessing meant that the waterlines required for each layer could now be drawn. However, even now great care had to be taken, as, in effect, the top half of the hull was a mirror image of the lower half. It is essential that each layer be cut to encompass the maximum width of that layer outside and the minimum width inside. With a "normal"

hull the maximum width occurs at the top of each layer and the minimum at the bottom. With this hull the shape above the armoured belt is the reverse. This is the sort of work that needs checking a couple of times before any timber is cut.

I always make each layer in two parts joined vertically through the keel. This allows the internals to be band-sawed out. This does two things: it lightens the hull and allows the hull to contract if it wishes, which avoids possible splitting. The vertical glued joint also acts as a built-in datum. You can also cut the base along the vertical keel and re-glue for the same reason.

# 22. The Bread and Butter Hull

## Part 2

With all the layers prepared gluing up can start. It is usual to start at the base. The secret is to make sure that the layers are glued up absolutely flat, without twist and in the correct relationship to each other. It is very easy to glue in errors of this type and ruin the hull. I always clamp the first layers to a known flat, untwisted surface until enough strength has been built up. **Fig.1** shows the first lifts being glued and held onto my building board. Wood is a natural substance and rarely remains absolutely flat and untwisted if left to its own devices.

Unfortunately, glue, whilst doing its proper job also acts as a first class lubricant and you will find, on applying pressure, the two surfaces will slide about destroying any correct relationships. You need to clamp them

**Fig 1. Lifts glued and clamped to building board to hold flat whilst glue cures.**

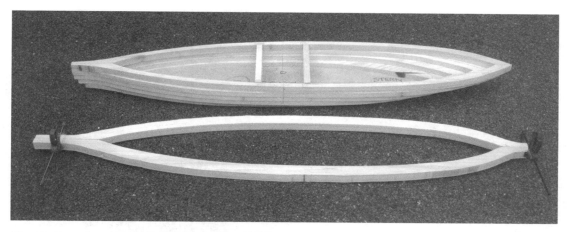

**Fig 2. An almost finished stack of lifts.**

up dry in the correct position and dowel them together. One eighth inch diameter wood dowels are quite strong enough for this job. Usually only two are required: one at the bow and one at the stern. If the sections are flimsy the beam may benefit from a couple as well. I always put a central transverse datum line on all sections and use this for fore and aft location. The vertical joins at the bow and stern are used for the transverse location. Choose the position of the dowels carefully. Either site them so they are totally in the scrap and will be removed or bury them in the hull never to be seen again. Do not use metal dowels and if any screws are used in the assembly process remove them. This is because Sod's law will ensure that wherever you put a screw will be exactly where you will need to drill a 0.5mm hole later on. **Fig.2.** The upper view shows the stack nearly finished. (Note the two transverse struts added to prevent the hull being crushed when held in the vice). The lower view shows a two-part layer being clamped and glued together before being added to the stack. Although I have never done so buttock lines can be used instead of waterlines. Buttock lines are vertical sections taken parallel to the keel instead of the horizontal sections called waterlines. Working with buttock lines produces a vertical collection of shapes

instead of the stack of shaped horizontal waterlines.

With the hull glued up the next stage is to remove the excess material. If you turn the model upside-down you have, in effect, a contoured shape with lots of protruding corners that have to be removed. I had the privilege of visiting the test tank at Feltham during its short life (it was demolished due to lack of work - this was the demise of the British shipbuilding industry). I saw how they made their water tank models. A very large block of paraffin wax was mounted on a machine table. Alongside was a drawing with all the waterlines on it. All the operator had to do was to set the height of the cutter relative to the block and follow a "waterline" on her drawing whereupon a high speed cutter would cut the same waterline in the block. This produced in wax what we have produced in wood.

The next stage is to smooth off all the corners to produce the finished shape. This is done by using templates at specific points along the hull to define the shape. I make my templates in stiff card marking their station on both sides for easy identification. It is a good idea to also mark at least one datum, say the load waterline, to ensure the template is applied in the correct vertical position. **Fig.3** shows the template against the nearly

**Fig 3. A template is used to check the carved shape for conformity.**

finished hull shape. There are several ways of making these templates. The classic ways are either to prick off the shape from your cross-section master drawing or to use carbon paper and trace it and then cut out the shape. Alternatively, scan the section drawings into the computer, I simply print the whole master drawing of the sections, as many times as there are stations, onto sticky-backed paper, stick them onto suitable card and cut out as usual. This saves time on what is often a fiddly and time-consuming job.

How you carve to the final shape is up to you; there is no "written in stone" way. Carvers quickly remove the rough stuff by using a gouge and a wooden mallet that is usually bell-shaped. This is known as bosting out. **Fig.4.** Their round shape means only one point of contact between mallet and tool handle, which avoids any bias when it strikes. Think about it.

When carving remember to carve with the grain. Normally, owing to the shape of the hull this will be from amidships toward the bow and toward the stern. However, wood being a natural material does not play by the rules and you may encounter grain running the opposite way to that expected. Do not panic, merely reverse your direction of attack over that area. Do not worry about minor imperfections or over-optimistic tool marks as these can be filled afterwards when the final finishing is carried out. I use "David's" Isopon P38 which I find works very well but other fillers are available. Polyfilla Fine Surface finish is excellent but only suitable for small imperfections as it sets by drying whereas two-part fillers cure chemically.

I always start amidships which establishes the basic shape. Cut the wood over a length of about three stations. Remember if your drawing office work is correct the correct shape of the hull lies at the interior corners between the layers. Your efforts are to ensure

## CHAPTER 22

**Fig 4. Initial carving using a chisel and mallet.**

the transverse profile between these datum points is correct, hence the use of templates. As your shape approaches finality ease off the rough stuff and use chisels, planes (if possible), Surform files, etc. to produce the required profile. As you get near the finished shape gradually extend the area of activity fore and aft where the shape gets more complicated especially at the stern where you may have double concave curves which can be difficult. The secret is to work slowly with frequent checking with templates but also by eye, looking at the work from all angles to ensure a clean line is maintained. Do not concentrate your efforts at one station until the adjacent stations are more or less finished. The shape should flow into correctness as it were!

When carving always remember the shape you seek lies somewhere in that block of material laying on the bench before you. It's your job, whether you be a humble chippy or Michelangelo himself, to find it. The problem with carving as opposed to modelling with clay, is once off it cannot be replaced so let that be your watchword.

# 23. Finishing the Hull
## Part 1

Features such as external armoured belts, torpedo bulges, etc are probably best left and added on afterwards.

You can of course put on an overall colour, white or grey, before any resin coat (my so-called rectification coat) as this will help to reveal any imperfections. It is very easy to miss any roughness, bumps or hollows with the grain camouflaging everything. It is

surprising how sensitive your fingers can be at exposing problems. If you watch car finishers they use their fingers more than their sight. However, a point to watch is if you are going to use a rectification coat **before** applying the two-part epoxy resin, make sure the two materials are compatible. These resin coatings are really designed for coating bare wood and may react badly with any previous undercoat. Although we are talking about bread and butter hulls what follows is largely applicable to all sorts of hull.

So we now have a completely carved hull finished off to a satisfactory finish. What now? Most hulls have fitments such as propeller shafts and rudders and now is the time to fit them before the painting proper. Any making good, which is inevitable (with me anyhow) can be done before final painting.

Fitting the rudder bearings usually presents no real problem except remember to drill the hole in the hull before finally fixing the lower support as, with this in position, you may need a very long drill to reach the hull. With my present hull for the French battleship Bouvet I made an extension piece in aluminium fixed with two machine screws into hidden nuts to provide the lower support

**Fig 2. Milling the slots in the A Frame bosses.**

**Fig 2. A Frame sub-assembly clamped into position on the hull.**

for the rudder. The lower rudder extension was far too flimsy to be carved from an extension of the wooden keel.

However, the propeller A-frames present a much more difficult problem and getting them in the right position and lined up correctly is often a nightmare. I remember quite a few years ago a friend coming down from Nottingham in the early hours to spend the day with me so I could fit a prop shaft to a GRP hull that I had made for him. He had chickened out.

To tackle this job, spend a lot of time on studying the plans to ascertain the position of the two legs of the A-frame and where the shaft enters the hull. Ship's hulls being largely strangers to straight lines finding the places to measure from can be difficult. Having decided where the holes should be do not start by drilling dirty, big holes all over the place as I find my first choice is always wrong and these will have to be filled. You thought I would always get it right first time but this is

not so. The hardware of the A-frame will also have to be made up. With the common type this usually involves a cylindrical bearing with two legs, which fit into the hull — when you get their position right that is. The first thing to remember is that the length of the legs that actually fits into the hull must be parallel otherwise you will not be able to slide them in or out of the hull. Annoying, ain't it? This presumes that the two legs are set at an angle in the bearing or boss thus producing the A-frame. The boss is usually a plain bored cylinder but may have pretensions to streamlining fore and aft. I always soft solder the legs into the slots in the boss, as that is one thing you can get absolutely right. **Fig.1** shows the blind slots being milled in on my milling machine. For interest the angle between the legs and hence the slots, was 86 degrees on this model. The slots were blind, i.e. not open ended, because the legs were narrower than the width of the boss. You can simply put saw cuts in to house the legs but you will have

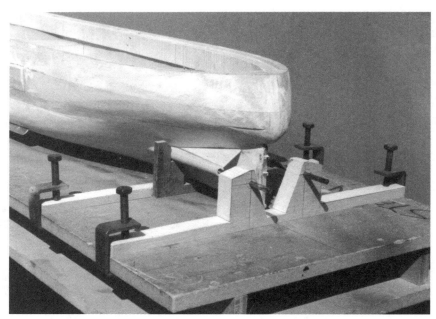

**Fig 3. Alignment of the shafts and A frames is a time consuming exercise but accurate results are obtained using a fixture such as this one.**

to fill up the redundant ends of the slots with solder or filler.

The next stage is to fit the completed A-frames to the hull in what you hope is the correct position. They won't, at least mine never do, first time anyway! You then start an investigation into why. This is usually done with a lot of heavy breathing and the removal of outer garments as I always start to glow at this point.

One aid to this problem is to drill holes through the legs and fit pins to act as depth stops so the penetration of the A-frames into the hull is fixed. **Fig.2**. These pins can be removed after assembly of course. After checking and re-drilling the holes if necessary you will get it right in the end. One problem is that being the superb modeller that you are you will drill the holes too tight. Open out the holes so the assembly can take up its natural position. This is no problem as glue and filler can be

used to finally set everything in place. **Fig.3** shows a fixture made of wood for lining up the shafts on my model of *RN Duilio*. You will note on this Italian ship the A-frame has been dispensed with as the prop shafts are totally enclosed.

Shafts can be set up without a fixture by using copious measuring and fiddling but more skill may be required. The time taken to make up a fixture is usually time well spent.

Incidentally the shaft enclosure at the hull end is best made from wood, as it has to be sharply tapered at its forward end to fit the surface of the hull. This fitment can be smoothed in with Isopon or a similar filler. All the above concerns the usual A-frame shaft arrangement found on British naval vessels. My present model is a three-screw vessel and the bearing supports for the two outboard screws are slightly different but the above method still applies.

# 24. Finishing the Hull
## Part 2

I had carved and finished the Bouvet hull ignoring the two armoured belts. The ship had a major armoured belt with a much thinner one on top. These were finally fixed by gluing and brass pinning. The pinning was necessary to make the wood strips follow the curve of the hull. Where the vertical section was nearly flat the belts could be laid as one piece. At the stern this was not so as the belt twisted and curved under the tuck of the hull. The vertical height was therefore split into three much narrower horizontal strips, which would conform, with a little persuasion, to the hull curvature. Bearing in mind my stricture on metal bits in the hull most of the

brass pins were removed after the adhesive had set. Those left in were punched under and the heads filled. **Fig.1** shows the lower edge of the main belt and the docking keels. So we have hung on all the bits and worked up a reasonable surface finish. The final job is to create yet another masterpiece with the paint job. **Fig.2** shows the final assembly of the A-frames, prop shafts, sternpost (rudder) and central prop shaft holes. At this point I always go into a minor decline; is the hull really ready? Do not add any paint until you are really sure that it is as good as you can get it. Look at it from every angle. Are all the bumps, lumps and bevel-edged pieces

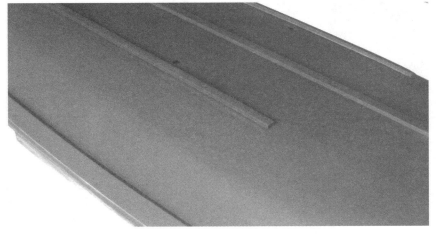

**Fig 1. To retain the sharp appearance of items such as belt and docking keels, painting has to cover but not obscure.**

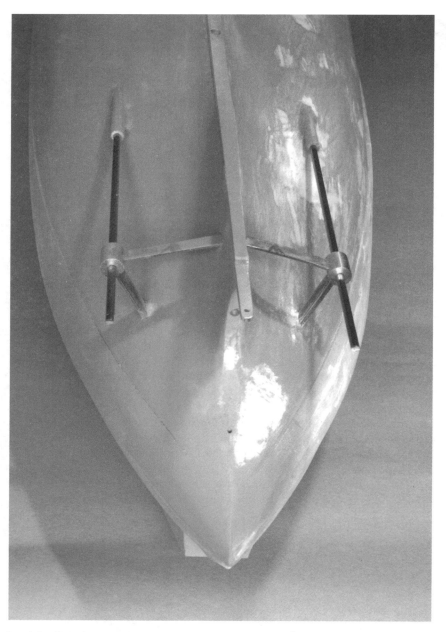

**Fig 2. A frames and central screw hole finished.**

banished? I always haul my hull out into the garden and shove it onto the top of my plastic water butt and there, at eye level, I challenge it to expose itself, if you will pardon the expression. You need to have it at eye level to be able to run your eye along its lines. Check that both sides are symmetrical. It

becomes a disaster if, for example, eventually the boot topping does not meet at the stem and/or stern. You should also make the rudder, as it needs to be painted at the same time as the hull for consistency. A rudder with a slightly different colour will look odd. Also check anything such as the rudder, which has to be fitted to the hull; that it does fit and allows for the thickness of the subsequent paint film. It is a disaster to have to remove the paint you have just put on to get parts to fit!

On my model of RN Duilio one of the propellers fouled the deadwood and very drastic measures, such as re-building the A-frame, had to be taken to correct the fault luckily before final coating. Make a point of excluding women, children, any maiden aunts and dogs from the workshop and its environs in case of bad language.

When you are convinced that everything is in physical order you can plan the final push to perfection. We really started this clambake talking about bread and butter hulls but finishing encompasses all hulls: GRP, vacuum formed plastic, or that rare item, a metal hull. Wooden hulls whether bread and butter or plank on frame can be coated with two-part epoxy resin. This has several advantages: it makes a stronger hull, it waterproofs and it provides an excellent surface for painting. Its disadvantage is that the resin can clog detail, fill up corners and "bead" edges. This may require correction.

GRP and plastic hulls should give no trouble except possibly de-greasing and fine roughing to provide a paint key for subsequent colour coats.

Metal hulls if made from steel (tin plate) may require anti-rust treatment such as coating with a zinc-based primer after de-greasing. Where water can be tolerated i.e. not wood hulls, de-greasing can be done with warm soapy water. Rubbing down or flatting is best done with wet and dry abrasive paper used wet. If used dry it may tend to burnish the surface rather than cut it. A little soap added to the rubbing down lubricates and makes the job easier but be very careful to remove all the "slurry" created before painting.

With wood hulls you cannot use liquid de-greasers. I use glass paper and keep my fingers off the surface as much as possible. Good adhesion of the primer to the original

surface and for all subsequent coats is essential to avoid paint rip-off when using masking tape. "Rip-off" is the bugbear of the finishing process and usually requires going back to basics - square one. It can be avoided by careful attention to correct procedures with no short cuts. Always use the best materials and take time over the whole process. The best masking tape I have found is the yellow tape supplied by Tamiya. It is expensive compared with others but as it is supplied in a plastic case its edges remain virginal (sorry about that!) and it does not require edge re-cutting as most others do. It also edge seals very well indeed, which avoids the other finishing headache – paint "bleed". Of course, the finishing on models has improved beyond measure over the last 20 years or so. I suspect this may be more to do with bought plastic hulls than with any great improvement in technique, however.

Those of you who bother to read my scribblings (incidentally, always done in my un-heated garret specially kept for such activity) will know of my war against dust. I make no excuse for touching on the subject again. It is essential to realise that it is always there even if you cannot see it. Cleaning off completely before any paint application is a must. Most modellers do not know about tack rags. These are used to finally remove dust before painting. They are not usually found in model shops but you can find them in car accessory shops. Otherwise use brushes and vacuum cleaners. Put clean newspapers over your benches, etc. This stops over spray contaminating the surface. Dust is OK if it is not disturbed and I do most of my spraying in my outside workshop which is even more dusty than my house but the light is superb as it has a glass roof. Incidentally when looking for hollows and lumps to fill, edge-light the subject as this will reveal imperfections far better than light coming over your shoulders. The same effect can be seen when flying – hills and valleys seem to disappear when they are beneath you.

# 25. Rudders

Rudders vary from a simple plate to more streamline shapes although the rudder on my model of RN Duilio has "panels" on it's surface, which tends to destroy the streamlining. On the prototypes the frame is usually a steel casting (note steel and not cast iron) sheathed with 15lb steel plating. In shipbuilding plate thicknesses are expressed in pounds weight per square foot e.g. a 10lb plate would be 1/4in thick and a 15lb plate would be 3/8in thick.

At the turn of the century (18th to 19th that is) the interior between the skins would have been filled with fir (pine wood) but a more suitable material is probably now used. Some rudders are simply top hung; the weight being taken by a bearing at the top of the sternpost. Such cantilever rudders are obviously more

**Fig 1. This rudder was built up from a folded brass etching and brass tube with filler added to refine the shape and fill gaps.**

**Fig 2. The gudgeons for the rudder are best added to the hull rather than cut out.**

liable to damage than rudders supported at both top and bottom. Therefore large rudders usually have a bearing at the bottom supported by an extension of the keel as well. Rudders can also be balanced or unbalanced. Balancing is achieved by pivoting the rudder back from its leading edge leaving a proportion of its area in front of the pivot. The pressure on this area balances, to some extent, the pressure on the rear part of the rudder when the helm is put over thus requiring less effort to turn it. This balanced effect is utilised when towing canal barges from the tow path. If the tow was attached to the point of the bow the barge would inevitably steer for the bank. As it is the towing point is about one third back from the bow. This has the effect of trapping water between the bow and bank, forward of the towing point, thus effectively stopping this. Over-balancing can be highly dangerous as the rudder may snap over to its extreme position immediately it is turned from its fore and aft position, its neutral position if you like. This would definitely be a "whoops sorry" situation! With aircraft this fault is likely to be lethal of course.

Conversely it can be seen that a large unbalanced rudder on a fast vessel would require a very powerful steering engine to turn it and to maintain its new position. I presume this is why you see several large steering wheels on sailing clippers whose rudders were unbalanced and lacked any form of power steering. Several very stout seamen were required at times to keep the vessel on course. On the model side various methods of construction are possible building it up or carving the thing from solid. I usually cut out the shape from Perspex and put on the "streamlining" with a file. In this case try and use an unused one as any previous use on metal will dull its cutting edges. The "panelling" on RN Duilio's rudder was an appliqué of thin plastic cut out to represent the recessed areas. On my present model I adopted a completely different method. **Fig.1.** This involved a piece of 0.008in brass shim of rudder height and more than twice its length. This was folded over to produce the leading edge of the rudder. One leg of the fold was the length of the rudder and the other was slightly longer. About one third back from its leading edge a vertical brass tube was trapped. The trailing edge was then soldered together and cleaned up. No attempt at shaping the longitudinal section was made apart from the initial leading edge fold. The streamline section required was a product of the method of its making. The brass tube was fixed with a touch of solder before folding up to keep it in its correct position. Allowing this sort of component a free hand always results in tears as their idea of correct position will not be yours! The tube provided a housing for the rudder shaft of course. To complete this type of rudder the open top and bottom were filled with Isopon or similar. If you want a little fullness behind the tube a piece of packing: cardboard, wood or whatever, can be inserted before doing the Isopon bit. This method produces a neat rudder with none of the tiresome filing required if the thing is hacked from a solid bit of sheet Perspex. I used a similar method on the etched wings and tailplane of the four types of aircraft I built for my model of the aircraft carrier HMS Glorious.

It is always a good idea to build the rudder at the same time as the hull and ensure they are sprayed at the same time to ensure continuity

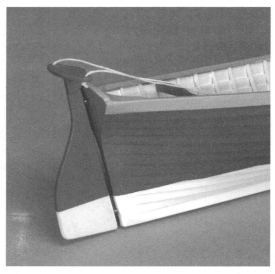

**Fig 3. Yoke equipped rudder with steering lines on the authors Scillonian gig.**

of colour and gloss but do make sure it fits properly before painting.

All the above really describes modern or large ship practice. Some rudders are mounted using pintles and gudgeons. This technique can be seen on small boats such as skiffs, cobles and the like. The pintle is the long pin(s) on the rudder which fits into the gudgeon(s) on the rudder post or stern of the boat. For stability's sake two or more are usually fitted. The pintles on the rudder usually cause no problems but cutting the gudgeons on a wood hull may be difficult. It is best to make these of brass on a separate piece half lapped and bolted to the hull. **Fig.2.**

For small ship's boats I usually etch the rudder, rudder shaft and tiller in one piece. Unless the boat is rigged as a sea boat the rudder is normally unshipped and lies in the stern sheets anyway. **Fig.3** shows a rudder equipped with a yoke and two steering lines on my six-oared Scillonian gig.

# 26. Propellers

In the previous column I discussed rudders at some length. In this column propellers are the topic; somehow they go together both being at the stern of the boat (usually) and the former directs the effort of the latter.

Today it is normal to cast propellers in one piece i.e. blades and boss are one unit. This is because we now understand the theory a little better and now have vertical water tunnels and the like to enable a study to be carried out. However, the Victorians did not have such tools to play with and matching props to ships, or vice versa, was a game of trial and error.

Many if not all their props consisted of three or four blades bolted to a separate boss. **Fig.1 and Fig.2.** This enabled the pitch of the blades to be altered within limits. I believe even into the thirties of the last century the propellers fitted to the liner *Queen Mary* had to

**Fig 1. A variable pitch propeller provides just a little more of a challenge. Note the finished gudgeon also visible in this photograph.**

**Fig 2. Another style of variable pitch propeller.**

be changed owing to excessive vibration. I remember when I was an apprentice visiting Stones of Deptford (I think it was) and being told that they had to use two very large crucibles pouring together so much molten bronze was required. Large propellers are certainly an expensive item.

Model props are usually made as separate blades and boss, soldered, either hard or soft, together. You can obtain proper monolithic (means all in one) props made using the lost wax casting method from at least one supplier in the UK. **Fig.3.** I use "Prop Shop" for mine but usually make my own metal blanks and do the final polishing.

For those not in the know this lost wax process in principle uses a built-up wax prototype, which is invested with a clay mixture. This is then fired to harden the clay and melt out the wax. Molten brass/bronze then fills the cavity evacuated by the wax and we should have a proper cast, all in one, propeller. The origins of this process lie in the mists of time but it is used a great deal in the jewellery business.

If the propeller shaft(s) is visible then I use stainless steel rod, which avoids rusting problems. Silver steel (centreless ground steel stock) can be used but it will rust if given half a chance. I always leave my prop shaft unpainted as I like the look of stainless steel. I remember Loren Perry pointing out at one ME that this was probably wrong and they should be painted. He is probably correct but I still leave mine unpainted. Incidentally if a stainless steel is called 18/8 it means 18% of the alloy is chromium and 8% is nickel. Household articles are usually of 18/8 but 18/10 is also used. Stainless steel is usually non-magnetic but this is not an infallible property as some are magnetic. However, if it proves to be non-magnetic and has that peculiar "grey" look it is a fair bet that it is stainless steel. A lot of Victorian battleships

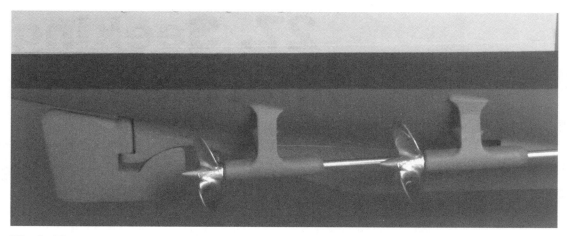

## CHAPTER 26

**Fig 3. Fine group of propellers, A frames and rudder.**

avoided the "is it painted or not" problem by enclosing the shaft right down to the propeller thus lubricating the propeller bearing. Most ships rely on sea water to lubricate the A-frame bearing which is often made from lignum vitae (Guaiacum officinale or G. sanctum). This is a very heavy resinous tropical wood. RNLI slip-launched lifeboats have forced lubrication to this bearing as they start their engines whilst still on the slip before entering the water. No one wants to start a rescue with a seized propeller!

Very small propellers (ship's boats for instance) can be a problem. If you are into etching they are a suitable subject to etch although a separate turned boss may also be necessary. Remember not to get the neck of the blade, where it connects to the boss, too narrow otherwise when twisting the blade into the appropriate helix it may shear off. Certainly etching saves a great deal of fiddly shaping work.

An alternative way, which does sound crazy I admit, is to twist them up from fine wire. I make up a little fixture comprising a central pin (the shaft in essence) and one for each blade i.e. two, three or four. You work out a system starting with the central pin winding on a turn (part of the boss) and then round each pin (the other part of the boss). After going round a "blade" pin you go back to the

"shaft" pin of course. Carefully remove this wirework from your fixture, twist each blade to a suitable angle and wipe a smear of PVA across each blade loop to fill it up. Blot up the "boss" and paint the PVA membrane over the blades with bronze paint. This produces a very fair representation of a *small* propeller. In my book "Advanced Ship Modelling" I go into this method a bit more fully. **Fig.4.**

**Fig 4. Very small propellers for ships boats can be made using wire and a painted PVA glue membrane.**

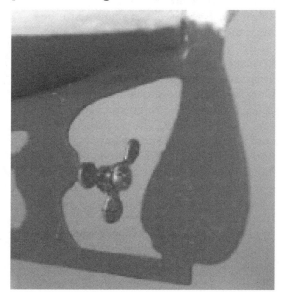

# 27. Seeking Information?

All model makers suffer from lack of detailed knowledge of what such things as capstans look like close-up. It is not until you sit down, or stand up, to make the part that you realise you do not know either. The broad outlines are clear but the detail information is not there; without that, fidelity to the original is just not possible. To the high-class modeller that is the all-important goal. I gave up making working models owing to pond-side pressure. Some details have to be sacrificed, as they will not stand up to the wear and tear imposed on the working model.

Let us look at where we can find the necessary information to build the part. Drawings vary enormously in the amount of detail shown. Some original drawings show very little fine detail. The position of a component may be shown but its detail may not. The late lamented Norman Ough often indicated a position for a component but left it at that. He did, however, also print a great deal of detail such as deck plank joggling, spar fittings, gun and turret drawings, etc. pertaining to current Naval practice at the time.

Admiralty (MOD) "as fitted" drawings vary enormously in their quality and the degree of information given. John Roberts says that drawings of the Dreadnoughts (1906) are very poor owing to the speed of building, which was only a year from keel laying to launch. Another fault, particularly with Victorian drawings is that they contain too much detail with layer on layer superimposed so that you are totally unsure of what any given line represents. One is tempted to think that their draughtsmen had too much time on their hands. In too many cases they also fail to show how high the objects are that are shown on the plan. This causes great difficulty.

So-called model maker's plans usually exclude extraneous detail and are therefore easier to read. Again they may vary in quality but often have a second sheet detailing many of the fittings, which is obviously a great help. The "Anatomy" books have masses of detail, which can also be used for other vessels of the same era.

All model makers should attempt to build a library around their interests. Collect anything appertaining to your interests. In time this becomes an essential tool in the pursuance of your hobby. Also cultivate friends of a similar persuasion as they can be of great help. Always return borrowed items if you wish to retain their friendship. Conversely check you get your loaned items returned as; when you need them you will not be able to remember where they are and who has them.

Plans are one thing but they may not be the complete answer to making a fitting especially if it is at all complicated. Photographs of the object may be essential as indeed they are for most modelled items. You may have photos in your own collection but if not where does one find them? Some museums have collections often not catalogued and only available at a price. However, beware of being told: "Yes we have a good collection of pictures of X". When you finally see the collection you may obtain some pictures of use but do not be surprised if you find "out of focus" and "camera shake" ruining most of the shots. Also photos taken against the light (contra jour) are usually pretty useless as most detail is hidden. Non-model makers can have no idea what you require. One curator I had dealings with thought that if I had a Norman Ough drawing I didn't need anything else. He was obviously one of those people who, on seeing a scratch-built model always have to ask: "Is it a kit?" Its one of those remarks that make me reluctant to show my work to the hoi poly. The other put down is: "I wouldn't have the patience to do that" meaning you must be an idiot.

Another technique for gleaning information on the shape of objects is to examine the shadow, if any, thrown by them. This sounds a little outré but it can work. In one picture I had, the outside accommodation ladder was not in its usual working position as the vessel was underway, so it was triced up horizontally at the deck edge. It only betrayed its presence by its shadow thrown onto the hull side otherwise it was, to all intents and purposes, invisible.

Yet another technique is to scan a photo into your computer and magnify the area under investigation. You will not get a nice sharp picture of course but it is surprising how you may be able to fathom out some detail not easily visible on the original.

Whilst discussing photos it should be pointed out that there is a world of difference between a proper photographic print and the same image printed in a book using the dot process. Magnifying the former is relatively easy and may prove fruitful whereas magnifying the latter often gets you nowhere except you get larger dots! With older pictures they may have been printed by the photogravure process, which does not use the dot matrix system and often produces a better magnified image.

A prolific source of valuable data is contained in the Admiralty Handbooks of Seamanship (HMSO). Mine came from second-hand bookshops. Try and obtain those pertaining to your period of interest. Those published early last century contain much information useful for modellers building Victorian era ships, such as details of the heavy stocked anchors that could not be housed up the hawse pipe but had to be laid onto built-in anchor beds. This method involved large cat davits to handle the anchors. All such detail can be found if you have these invaluable books. If, like me, you have several different periods of interest you can see the gradual development of the Royal Navy. For instance the 1915 copies do not refer to aircraft carriers - I don't know why.

Another valuable soured of information, at least for the Victorian era, is the Navy and Army Illustrated volumes of which were published in the late 19th century as bi-weekly issues. A binding facility must have been available as, surprisingly; bound copies are still available on the second-hand book market. The best volume that I have ever seen is Vol. 1 (dated Friday Dec 20th 1895 to June 12th 1896 with a couple of special extra issues thrown in). This volume contains a large number of photos of naval vessels of the time and a fair number of onboard shots showing much detail. These pictures were taken with big cameras producing large glass plate images, which were printed size, and not blown up, as we would have to do today with 35mm cameras. The Victorian lenses may not have been very good but the lack of enlargement still gives a fairly sharp result – good enough for the likes of us anyway! My copy of this volume, which had been my beloved grandfather's, eventually, fell to pieces because I used it so much. A very good friend, now unfortunately also departed, rebound it in leather so I still have it, both for its contained information and as a reminder of two dear people.

An interesting point is that some, at least, of these negatives may still be in existence somewhere as you occasionally come across some of these images reprinted in modern books. It is noticeable that the images have degraded over the years unless the contemporary pictures are the result of many copies of copies being taken. One

disadvantage is that many of the onboard shots are filled with jolly jack tars in various attractive poses, hands on hips, etc. They certainly were not taken for the edification of the modelling fraternity who are far more interested in what the aforesaid sailors are hiding. The evidence suggests that our Victorian forebears were not into model making. It is surprising how many sources of information are available to you if your own collection fails you.

Two other valuable sources of information are "Navy News" published monthly by the Navy, which mainly deals with current goings on but occasionally covers things past. Last but by no means least, Dave Wooley's monthly column in Model Boats magazine always has masses of information and pictures of modern warships and fittings.

# 28. Anchors

## Part 1

If one studies the anchor problem one is faced with a plethora of choices from stones with holes in them, through the era of stocked anchors to really modern types neatly housed in their own depressed housing on the bow. Incidentally this practice, apart from looking shipshape and Bristol fashion, stops rough seas from hitting the flukes and spraying all over the bows. However, you can really sort them into five classes although there may be endless variations on a theme produced by different manufacturers. Admiralty pattern anchor **Fig.1** Stocked anchor requiring an anchor bed.

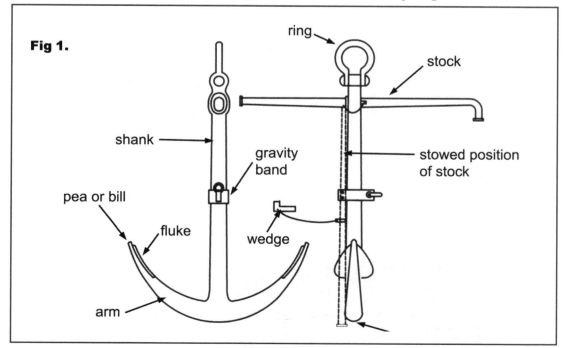

Fig 1.

ring

stock

shank

gravity band

stowed position of stock

pea or bill

fluke

wedge

arm

**Fig 2. A Victorian stocked anchor settled onto its bed. Fig 3. (opposite page) A modern stocked anchor.**

**Fig.2**
Early stockless anchor capable of being pulled up into a hawse hole **Fig.3**
Modern stockless anchor **Fig.4**

# Danforth and CQR anchors

**Type 1**. The Admiralty pattern anchor is the anchor seen (usually fouled with rope) on badges, etc.

**Fig 5. Many Victorian warships carried as many as 4 anchors in the bow plus further anchors amidships.**

**Type 2**. Victorian anchors were certainly focal points as they lived on anchor beds or were stowed vertically on the ships hull at the stern. **Fig.5**. Victorian ships carried as many as four on the bows with two on the stern and possibly Admiralty pattern anchors stowed amidships. I think they had a dread of being stranded off a lee shore, a remembrance of sailing ships with no power being wrecked thus.

**Type 3**. The early stockless anchor saved a lot of complication as without the stock it could be drawn up into the hawse hole and thus required no anchor beds, their associated handling gear or number of large cat davits to lift them up into position, all of which cluttered up Victorian fore decks more than somewhat.

**Type 4**. The modern stockless anchors are versions of type 3. In 1943 the Admiralty initiated a series of tests to improve the efficiency of anchors i.e. improving the ratio between weight of anchor and holding pull. The resultant AC12 and AC14 designs have a ratio of 1:10, much improved over previous designs. They all work on the same principle in that on being dragged along the weight of the flukes combined with the effect of the tripping palms forces the flukes into the sea bed. The tripping palms are extensions to the head at right angles to the flukes, which have the effect of rotating the head and hence the flukes into the sea bed.

**Type 5**. The Danforth is a new design suitable for use in small vessels. It is like a lightly built stockless anchor but because the flukes are relatively close together it has a small stock at the crown to prevent rolling but this does not impede its stowage in a hawse pipe.

The CQR anchor has a "plough" fitted to its bent shank. It is not easy to stow but useful for small craft.

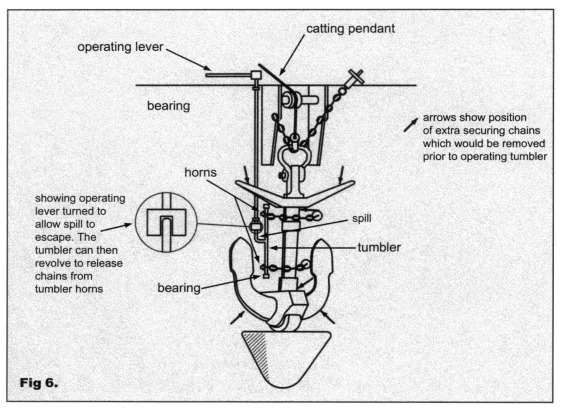

operating lever

catting pendant

bearing

arrows show position
of extra securing chains
which would be removed
prior to operating tumbler

horns

showing operating
lever turned to
allow spill to
escape. The
tumbler can then
revolve to release
chains from
tumbler horns

spill

tumbler

bearing

**Fig 6.**

All the above anchors except **Type 1** have the head pivoted on the shank. This movement is controlled by stops cast in the head. This limited movement is necessary to allow the flukes to operate. The model maker must either use a pivot or fix the shank at an angle to the head. I usually fit mine into the hawse hole and adjust the angle between head and shank so that the head sits snugly against the hull side. Putting in a proper working pivot is not easy.

## Anchor release mechanisms

For those interested in Victorian battleships and models thereof the tumbler release mechanisms for both anchor bed and vertically stowed anchors will be of interest. **Fig.6** shows the arrangement used for a vertically stowed anchor and **Fig.7** shows the method for an anchor supported on an

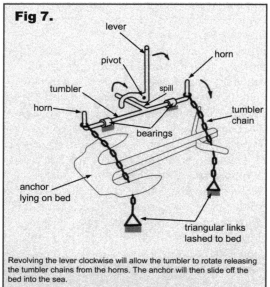

**Fig 7.**

lever

pivot

horn

tumbler

spill

horn

tumbler
chain

bearings

anchor
lying on bed

triangular links
lashed to bed

Revolving the lever clockwise will allow the tumbler to rotate releasing the tumbler chains from the horns. The anchor will then slide off the bed into the sea.

**Right: aft anchor as fitted to HMS Magnificent.**

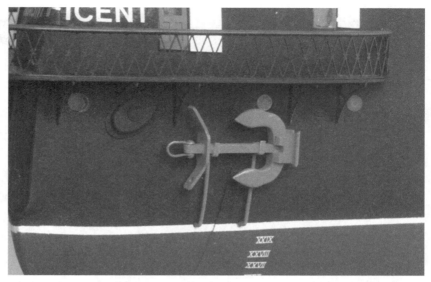

anchor bed. It will be noted that the release mechanism is similar in both cases. Turning the operating lever releases the two main holding chains simultaneously allowing gravity to take over. For safety extra restraints consisting of rope lashings also secure the anchors in both cases. These have to be cut before releasing the anchors of course.

As the orientation of the anchors is different the methods of hoisting are also different. The vertically stowed is hoisted via a catting pendant on its shackle whereas the horizontally stowed are lifted via their gravity bands. These bands are sited at the anchor's centre of gravity and ensure that it remains horizontal when hoisted.

# 29. Anchors

## Part 2

## Making Model Anchors

I use plastic for this job either Perspex sheet or a material called Tufnol of which there are several grades. Tufnol consists of layers of paper (cheaper grades) or cloth impregnated with the artificial resin phenol formaldehyde or similar. The reinforcement of paper or fabric makes it very strong and it is an ideal material for this sort of work. MOD (Ministry of Defence) drawings, certainly of Victorian vintage, usually show the anchors and the manufacturers name together with the weights of both the sheet and bower. (The bower anchors are the largest anchors carried

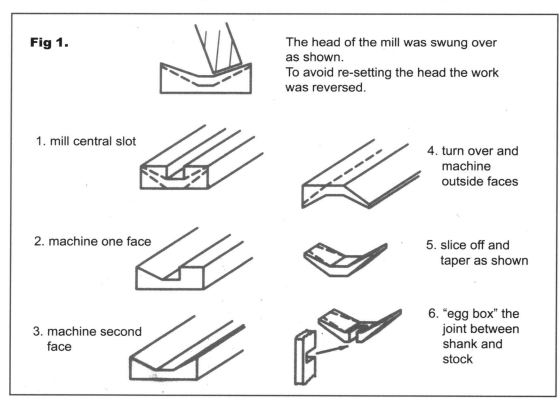

**Fig 1.**

The head of the mill was swung over as shown.
To avoid re-setting the head the work was reversed.

1. mill central slot

2. machine one face

3. machine second face

4. turn over and machine outside faces

5. slice off and taper as shown

6. "egg box" the joint between shank and stock

by the ship. The third bower anchor is called the sheet anchor and is usually not quite as heavy as the others. It is really a standby anchor). This drawing information can be abstracted and the anchors shaped. Long experience has taught me not to mark out plastic but to stick on a sticky label with the shape drawn/printed on it. You get a much clearer line to work to this way. The shape can then be fret-sawed out. Tufnol being a thermosetting resin will cut easier than Perspex, which tends to melt and clog the blade. The shank of the anchor is usually of a rectangular or square section and may be slightly tapered with the head end being larger than the shackle end. In some cases the section may be circular but in any case it should not be any trouble to make. The stock may be more difficult. Some stocks can be made from metal or plastic sheet as they are of constant thickness. I use aluminium or brass according to what is to hand. Some stocks, however, are tapered in thickness and will

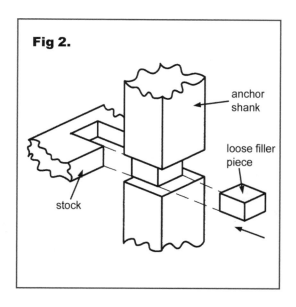

Fig 2.

need machining as shown in **Fig.1**, which gives the sequence of machining required. Make up a length and slice off pieces; do not machine each individual stock. The plan view

## Fig 3. The classic wooden stock anchor.

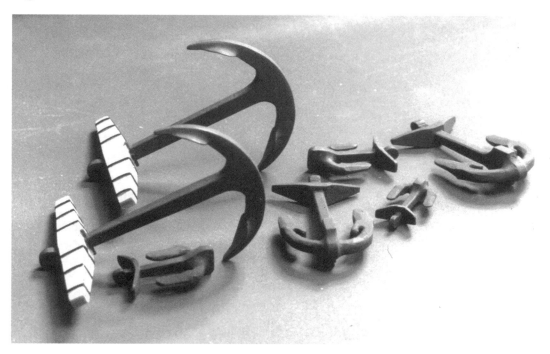

**Fig 4. Simple mould cast from silicon rubber for mass-producing anchors.**

is also usually tapered and each end may have a pierced hole, which should cause no trouble. Fixing the stock to the shank can be difficult. The simple way is to cut an appropriately shaped hole to fit the shank. This hole can be simply a round, drilled hole squared out with a small square file. A metal cutting fretsaw (if appropriate) can be used after drilling a hole for the blade or, if you require a square hole with round corners drill out the four corners with the correct sized drill and fretsaw or file the rest. This will give no positive location along the shank however, particularly if it is tapered slightly. An alternative way is to put three grooves around the shank and a slot in the stock and slide together as shown in **Fig.2**, adding a separate piece to close the gap. This sounds more difficult than it is to do but provides a positive location between the two pieces. A junior hacksaw gives the right sized slot.

The classic two-part tapered wood stock as shown in **Fig.3** was clenched to the shank by the metal bands, enclosing the stock, being forced up the taper towards the shank.

Therefore the two extreme ends of the wood parts will be in close contact but along the rest of the joint there should be a tapered gap to ensure that they are being forced tightly against the shank. If you do not read me have another think!

All anchors are equipped with a shackle, which I make from brass wire. I use 1/32in round-headed brass rivets about 1/4in long as the securing pin. These are about the smallest easily obtainable rivets and are supplied by nearly every trader in the model engineering field. I secure them by putting a blob of epoxy on the free end. You can, if so minded, make up a loose head and secure it with cyano or epoxy but this is not usually necessary.

Incidentally getting smaller rivets than these is difficult and you have to find a specialist supplier to do so but it is surprising how useful a supply of 1/32in brass round-headed rivets are in boat building.

Anchors on models pay for attention as they are always a prominent addition to a model. If you have to design a symmetrical shape

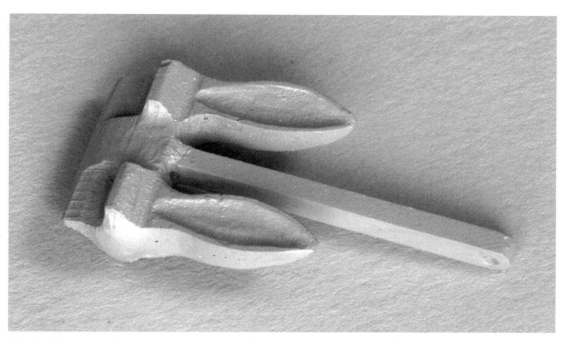

## CHAPTER 29

**Fig 5. The resultant resin-cast anchor,**

and this goes for anything, not only anchors, and you have a drawing programme in your computer only draw half of the component and mirror it. In this way you get perfect symmetry without hassle. Print this on sticky paper, which is readily available. If you have no computer draw half the anchor on folded sticky paper and cut it out. Using a computer saves time and improves accuracy.

With the blanks sawn out and cleaned up with a fine file you are nearly there. Note which parts are rounded off and which left fairly sharp. Remember the originals were cast and so shapes should flow into each other. Some anchors had recesses cast in the face of the flukes. These are probably best put in with a dental burr. I find it easier if the burr is rotating very fast. At slower speeds they can "walk" and show wilful behaviour, which may not be what you want.

With Admiralty pattern anchors you have the choice of exhibiting it with the rod shaped stock in place or lying parallel to the shank.

You will note the stock has a knob on the ends and a "shoulder" about half way along itself. This shoulder locates against the shank and is held there by a key hammered into a slot on the opposite face of the shank. These knobs and shoulders are difficult to make as the obvious way is to use a piece of wire for the stock. I use a technique learned during my apprenticeship and we won't go in to how long ago that was. Tin the end and shoulder area with soft solder in the normal way, cool the job down and load up your iron with solder. With a quick dabbing movement deposit solder onto the tinned areas. Repeat until you have built up somewhat knobbly deposits. These can then be turned on a lathe to produce the required knobs and shoulder. The secret is to keep the work absolutely cold. If you allow it to heat up the build-up will melt and run off. It is a technique that can be quite useful. You will need to put on the knobs and shoulder before putting in the right-angled bend required on the stock of an

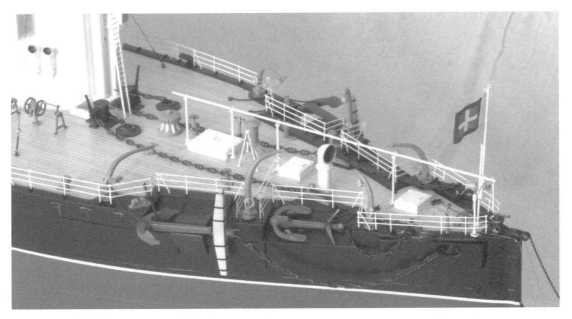

**Above: Anchors fitted to Duilios bow.**

Admiralty pattern anchor. With this type of anchor the actual flukes or palms are made of sheet metal and glued to the arms. They need to be radiused into the arms with polyester paste (Isopon or the like). If you are etching these can be etched which is easier than trying to cut small pear-shaped pieces of metal. With the CQR anchor I see no other way of making the "plough" part but to bend it up from sheet brass. It would be a nice little exercise for a Sunday afternoon – make a template in cardboard or, better still, lithoplate to get the shape right.

If several anchors of the same type and size are required you can make a blank and from that a silicon rubber mould. As many anchors as needed can then be cast in resin and they will all be the same. **Figs.4 and 5.**

# 30. Problems, Problems!

The essence of modelling is to translate the prototype, be it ship, aircraft or whatever to a miniature version of itself often employing entirely different materials and techniques. For instance, I have very little Harveyed armoured steel plate in my workshop. The skill of the scratch builder, in particular, is to translate what the builder's drawings tell him into materials and methods he can adopt to produce his model. With kits this process has been done by the kit designer as he has to supply said materials, instructions and plans. The latter may, in fact, differ significantly in detail from the original, although still making up into a fair model.

An example of this is my present model of the French pre-Dreadnought battleship Bouvet. There are model maker plans for this ship as well as the real McCoy in the shape of a set taken from the "as fitted" dockyard plans. All the turrets on this ship are slightly oval in plan shape whereas on the model makers plan they are shown as circular which means they can be turned. Turrets, which are not circular, present a big increase in workload. In this case the "oval" shape is made up from two circular curves. The smaller ones, spaced apart, produce the ends with a larger curve joining them together tangentially as shown in **Fig.1.** I found it easier to produce the three oval shapes required on the computer which, damn it, can draw more accurately than me. These shapes were printed on sticky-backed paper, cut out, and stuck onto the correct thickness of wood, roughly band-sawed to shape and finally disc sanded down to the thin line on the paper. I ensured the major and minor discs of the oval were retained as I needed to pick these up when boring for the barrel, fitting the large sighting hood, etc. With such shapes which are nearly circular but ain't, if

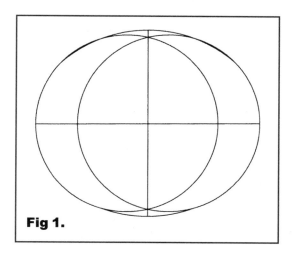

**Fig 1.**

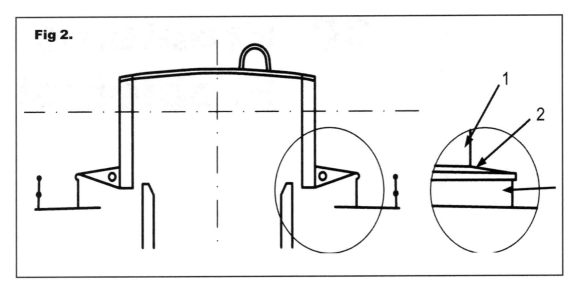

Fig 2.

you lose your datums things can get difficult. However, although that solved one problem the main one was how the deuce did the main turret system work. Being french it certainly did not follow RN practice. It took some time and much looking at plans before the penny, franc or euro dropped. In essence, as can be worked out from **Fig.2**, surrounding the turret was a light vertical bulkhead concentric with the point of rotation. Fixed to the turret proper and therefore rotating with it was a "skirt" which fitted over this bulkhead and prevented the ingress of the 'oggin which would otherwise pour down the sides of the barbette. OK, problem solved – but how to make the assembly, particularly the skirt. To complicate the matter further the turret itself was mounted offset. The point of rotation was nearer the barrel end of the oval presumably to act as a counter weight to the longer than usual (British practice that is) gun barrel. Perhaps the French were using a slower burning propellant thus requiring a longer barrel. One complication was eliminated as this was to be a glass-case model it did not need to rotate. Always fix things down on cased models otherwise you find that after a long journey things have forgotten their place and

moved, necessitating removal of the case – always a two man job. This process is always a heart-stopping occasion. My late wife, of happy and beloved memory, hated this process and threatened to go into a decline at the mere thought.

The top of the skirt where it attached to the side of the turret was shown as a horizontal line. If you are still with me this meant that the slope on its top surface altered throughout 360degrees as its width varied. This meant it could not be turned although its outer edge was a true circle. Therefore this piece was made from 2.5mm thick basswood, which could be carved to shape. This skirt was glued to a Tufnol disc, which represented the vertical bulkhead previously mentioned as well as the overhanging lip of the skirt. This lip detail needed to be kept sharp and clean, hence the use of Tufnol (plastic impregnated cloth or paper) for this part which also supported both skirt and turret proper. Perspex could also have been used for this. Looking at **Fig.2** the left-hand view is a section through the builders drawing. The right hand view shows how the original was modified: 1 is the turret proper, 2 is the basswood skirt, and 3 is the vertical bulkhead and the sealing edge of the skirt.

## CHAPTER 30

The point of all this is to show care must be exercised in the choice of materials bearing in mind you have to make the thing. If I had made the skirt in, say plastic, the problem of putting that constantly changing slope on its upper surface would have been a nightmare – it would probably have turned my hair grey! The result is something that externally looks like the prototype but has been produced in an entirely different way. With this type of work it usually pays to not do what was done with the prototype but to examine the problem from your point of view. I always draw it out first, to ensure I have remembered everything.

I suppose if you have had training and experience as a production engineer you tend to look at things from that point of view. A couple of examples. When R.J. Mitchell designed that beautiful aircraft, the Spitfire, he put double curvature in his fuselage metal covering whereas Willie Messerschmitt with his 109 had a simple one-piece single curvature covering his tail. Just think of the extra work involved! We will not mention the problems with the elliptical wings. The firm of Airspeed before WW2 built the Queen Wasp radio controlled target practice aircraft.

This was a biplane seaplane with tapered wings, think of it, every wing rib a different shape. Compare this with the wing of the V1 – a plain rectangular wing shape – cheap and easy to make. Looking at the design of many things particularly those things that will probably have a very short life one is appalled at the unnecessary complication designed into them. On the other hand everyday things such as coffee jar lids, impact produced containers and ring pull cans, are marvels of production engineering which most of us ignore completely.

Model makers need to exercise their brains just as athletes exercise their bodies. We mostly look but we do not observe. Look at things; how were they made and why were they designed that way? Get into the habit of using your brains because that way you develop flexibility and new ideas form, usually at 2 o'clock in the morning, but form they do. Try and work out how a plastic injection moulded jar lid is made, remembering the number required and the fact that it has an internal thread! So how do you get it out of the mould and what is the significance of the single or double digit number on the inside of the lid? Think on!

# 31. Decking

I've had a query about the decking for a proposed model of the battleship Rodney from my friend Greg Metcalfe so I thought I would use it as an excuse for a Column. Firstly it should be said that perhaps decking is the Achilles heel of model making because you see a lot of errors even, dare I say it, on museum models. Decks can be made from plywood simply lined out with pencil or ink - if that is good enough for you. But, a properly laid deck made up from separate planks is really the only way to do the job and once you have made such a deck, lined plywood will never be your choice again - believe me.

However, there are Admiralty, rules, which are largely ignored by modellers. For instance, the arrangement of the butts is important. The rules state that there must be at least three unbroken planks between a pair of butts. This is known as 3-butt planking. You can also have 4-butt planking with four unbroken planks between butts.

I always make my decks from basswood (American Lime), which can be obtained in very accurately cut sheets. I use basswood because it has no grain pits and presents a smooth surface. It tends to "string" when cut but this can easily be cleaned off. You need the accuracy because the thickness of the sheet becomes the width of the plank. Paint one side with black paint. Use a very dark grey (I use Tamiya Nato black) rather than pure black as black tends to "shout". Cut off lengths of your sheet corresponding to a scale length of 20 - 25ft and paint one cut edge. If you now slice off your planks to a thickness of 1mm, or whatever, you will have planks with one edge and one end already caulked (the black paint). I always lay them with the caulking on the starboard side and aft end to avoid two thicknesses of caulking coming together. You will note, if you are still with me, the original sheet thickness has become the plank width. The thickness of the plank produced by the slicing/sawing process is not very critical as the finished laid deck will need cleaning up anyway.

I start by laying a line of planks along the centre line and then abut subsequent lines of planks to it either side. Each line of planks need to be spaced along a quarter of the length of the already laid plank as will all subsequent plank lines. This will give you a 3-butt deck. If you want a 4-butt deck the spacing becomes one fifth. You can see this in **Fig.1**. **Fig.2** shows the planks joggled into the margin planks. You will note that no plank

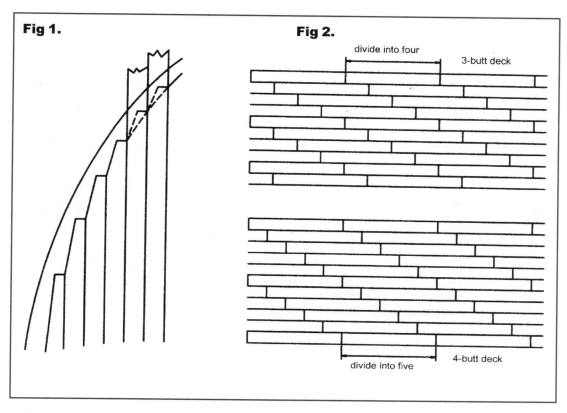

**Fig 1.**

**Fig 2.**

divide into four

3-butt deck

divide into five

4-butt deck

ends in a point which, in practice, would be impossible to secure. The flat is half the plank width. The rule states that if the snape, the tapered bit, is longer than twice the plank width then it has to be joggled into the margin plank. My observation is that joggling was carried out in many cases with the snape less than twice as long. Otherwise the plank was simply laid abutting the margin plank and not joggled in.

This is how I start the planking but I have no idea how dockyard mateys do it. With my method the butts along the centre line do not quite give you a 3-butt deck but the rest of the planking does.

A word about plank widths. Modern planking uses planks about 6in wide or even less. The planking on Victory is about 12in wide. I always plank my Victorian ships with wider planks than would be used today for the simple fact that timber of that quality was

still available then. Also photographs of the period enable you to compare sailor's feet with the plank width. Judges will dock you marks for this but that's their problem, not mine.

All this works with planks above about 1.5mm but thinner planks become difficult to lay and another technique is required. Battleship models at a scale of 1:192 require planks of 1mm width. In this case you prepare your timber as before but in this case laminate 4 thin sheets together after painting one side of each sheet. This needs to be done very carefully to ensure an accurate flat laminate. I sandwich the laminate between flat heavy surfaces. This laminate can then be laid as strips of four planks. You will not get any butts of course but they can be put in afterwards with an "H" grade pencil. One problem is that the strips of laminate must be longer than any length found on the model's deck. This is because you cannot join your

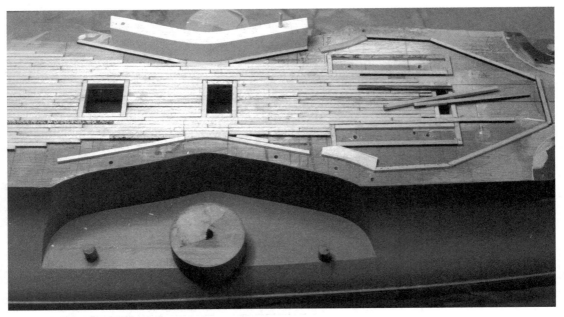

**Above: Planking in progress on the deck of Bouvet.**

strips of 4 planks because you would then get 4-butts in a line – which is not required.

I hope that helps Greg but I would add the decks on Rodney and her sister ship Nelson were made of fir (I presume this means pine) and not the usual teak. This was to keep the weight down; necessary because of the naval treaties being signed at that time.

You need to think about how you are going to clean up the planking after laying. You cannot have upstanding margins to the deck as this would preclude cleaning off the surface or at least make it very difficult. I use an adjustable mouth plane with the mouth closed right up, which should avoid tearing when planing against the grain. Needles to say the blade should be very sharp.

I deal with deck planking probably to a greater degree than above in my first book Advanced Ship Modelling (SI Books).

# 32. Gun Barrels

In a previous Column I discussed main armament and the difficulties of turning the tapers on gun barrels and the like. Having just turned 12 main armament gun barrels for my model of the French pre-Dreadnought battleship Bouvet I thought I might return to the subject as gun barrels are such a conspicuous feature of warships. Bouvet showed the typical mixture of gun calibres that were "cleaned" up in Fisher's HMS Dreadnought whose main armament was all of one calibre making gun control easier. Bouvet's main armament was of three calibres all mounted singly in oval turrets.

Another modelling nightmare – why not circular, a nice turning job? These French guns seem to have a larger diameter/length ratio i.e. were "thinner" than their equivalent British types and hence more difficult to machine. As explained in my previous column turning between centres is the classic way of machining long cylinders but the support provided by the lathe centres is inferior to holding the left hand end in the lathe chuck whilst supporting the overhanging end by the tailstock. We engineering blokes talk about the left hand end being "encastre" i.e. "embedded" in the chuck, therefore that end

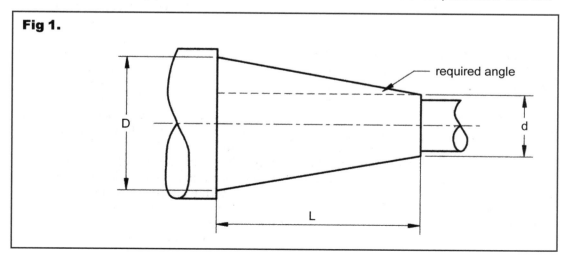

**Fig 1.**

required angle

D

d

L

**Fig 2. Bouvet gun barrel supported on a reversed drill during turning.**

can only move by bending the job itself outside the confines of the chuck so the set-up is stiffer. Turning a cylinder between centres tends to produce a barrel shape as the work is progressively pushed away by the tool as it approaches the centre of the length. Remember the tool deflects the work away in the horizontal plane and upwards in the vertical plane. Most of us with any experience at all will have had the upsetting experience of finding a piece of small diameter turning suddenly climbing up on top of the rake face of the tool. Quite puts one off ones dinner! Coming back to Bouvet, about time I hear you say, as I had no detailed drawings of the three guns in question dimensioned sketches had to be prepared from available views on the main drawings supplemented by looking at photos of the ship. Select a drawing that looks reasonable and mark it as the reference. Put dimensions of diameters and lengths on your sketch and check these a couple of times. Do not make a mistake at this point as it is likely to waste much time and material if you get it wrong.

You will then need to calculate the angles of the taper to enable the top slide to be set. Whilst the parallel portions of the barrel can

be turned using the "self act" i.e. the powered lead screw/feed shaft screw, the tapers will require manual operation of the topslide which will reveal how good a turner (or vice versa) you are!

The calculations are simple: divide half the difference between the diameters by the length and find the angle represented by the tangent of that number. Or more simply: $(D-d)/2 \div L = (D-d)/2L$. **Fig.1**. If you have a calculator with trig signs do the arithmetic calculation, push the inverse button and then the tan button, which should produce the angle required. However, the angle found usually needs to be increased slightly to compensate for the "spring" in the system. If this trig is beyond you perhaps your wunderkind can do it for you? Now that education is not compulsory he/she may not, in which case draw it out about 10 times full size and measure the angle with your trusty protractor.

**Fig.2** shows an overhead shot of my Myford set up for turning the muzzle end of the smallest of the three Bouvet gun barrels. The points to notice are the reversed drill held in a pin-chuck which is in turn held in the normal tailstock drill chuck. You will see the quill of

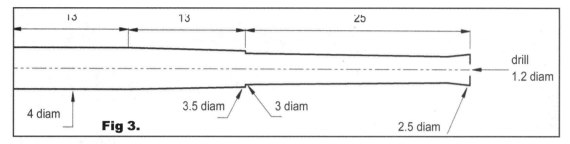

## CHAPTER 32

**Fig 3.**

the tailstock is quite extended to allow the angled topslide access to the job. The taper on the job will be put on using the topslide. This arrangement is far from satisfactory as although the left hand support is as firm as the headstock bearings will allow, the right hand end has capacity for much "spring". The combination of the drill supporting the muzzle bore, the pin chuck, the larger drill chuck, the extended quill detract from rigidity but this is still better than allowing the slender muzzle end freedom, if you get my drift. The pin chuck is necessary if the tailstock chuck will not close sufficiently to hold the small drill.

**Fig.3** shows a dimensioned scale drawing of the smallest main armament gun barrel. Note the two tapered lengths and the muzzle swell at the right hand end. With the amounts of taper found we can proceed after re-checking the information. Any errors here can result in much time and material being wasted. A point to remember is that such waste can affect you psychologically as well, in that your enthusiasm for the job can be severely weakened. Turning a bunch of gun barrels can be hard work and getting them all right can be a great boost in a long job. Vice versa can be a disaster! Remember that each taper, once correctly set, needs to be performed on all parts before passing on to the next operation. This means the job has to be removed and replaced in the chuck several times. To ensure maximum concentricity the part needs to be replaced in the chuck in the same place. Get into the habit and this is a good one, of marking the work at the No1 jaw position and replacing the work back in

the chuck observing the marks. It is very easy, well it is for me, to forget this and haphazardly replace the work in any old position only to find it isn't concentric anymore. This usually results in a sore toe where you have kicked the furniture.

Anyway – to horse- Operation sequence:

1.　Face centre and drill bore (in this case 1.2mm diameter)

2.　Reverse, face to length, 51mm, and centre (this is for tailstock support later)

3.　With muzzle end in lathe chuck, with about 30mm extended, free end supported by the centre in the tailstock turn 4mm diameter by 26mm long

4.　Reverse and hold on 4mm diameter, turn 3mm diameter by 25mm long with muzzle supported by 1.2mm diameter drill reversed in tailstock chuck (LUBRICATE drill)

5.　With topslide set to correct angle turn taper but leave about 3mm long at the muzzle still at 3mm diameter

6.　Turn this 3mm length down to the muzzle swell diameter, in this case 2.8mm and the endeavour to turn in the swell curve. I rough it out using the normal turning tool and finish it off with a round-nosed form tool. I have to admit turning in this swell curve is not easy and requires practice as using any kind of form tool on a small lathe almost always causes the turner's nightmare – chatter. Once chatter has marked the work it tends to be self-repeating and can only be overcome by experience. Try moving the tool sideways slightly whilst advancing the cut. If this does not work use a half round file to both work out the chatter and put in the curve.

# 33. Computers and Modelling

## Part 1

I should first state that I do not like computers and they don't like me! I find them wilful, unreliable and all in all a pain in the rear end. Alan Turing has an awful lot to answer for.

Having said that they can help the modeller in all sorts of ways and this column is an attempt to show you how I use my computer together with its associated scanner, printer and camera.

This article will be typed into the computer, checked, altered and generally messed about before the illustrations are added and the whole thing sent electronically to the publisher. The ease with which one can alter text compared with the typewriter is very apparent.

The ability of the computer to enlarge or reduce can be exploited when changing scales. For example, drawings of ship's boats given in the "Anatomy" series of books are very

**Fig 1. Component locations for rear bridge of Bouvet are printed onto sticky backed paper to aid positioning.**

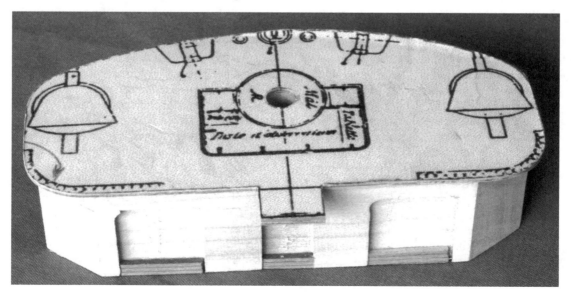

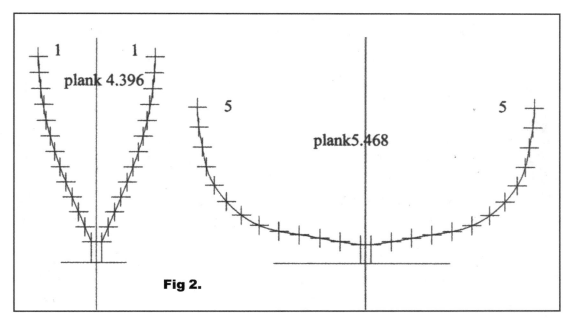

**Fig 2.**

useful but will always be drawn to the wrong scale for your model. If you have a scanner these can be scanned and the computer can give you prints to your selected size. This avoids having to go down to the local photocopy shop and find out their machine won't do the job anyway.

Allied to this is the ability of the system to print drawings on to sticky-backed paper or transparent sheet to any scale. This is a good and accurate way of transferring original drawing detail to wood, plastic, etc for cutting out and component positioning. **Fig.1** shows this technique applied to the rear bridge on Bouvet. Not only did it indicate the shape to be cut out but shows features such as the position of the two 100mm guns, their ready use ammunition racks, three smaller weapons and the rear mast with its surrounding superstructure.

An unorthodox use of the computer is to scan actual photos or pictures in books and to blow them up on the screen. The quality may be terrible but you can often see things not normally visible. Old pictures have often been printed in what I think was a process called photogravure and not the more modern dot matrix system. Pictures produced by this process yield to magnification on the computer. Moiré patterns sometimes show up but often further magnification gets over this problem. By altering the lighting and contrast on these scans sometimes previously unseen detail becomes visible.

The digital camera has become a very useful tool for taking shots of ships or parts thereof, fittings, etc for future reference. Unlike film cameras instant access to the shot is possible. The computer usually becomes part of the printing and viewing process and can be used for any manipulation of the image.

A computer with the correct software installed will enable digital pictures to be altered/corrected in all sorts of ways. Cropping and altering the "lay" of the image can be undertaken as well as lightening, darkening or changing the contrast. If you can think it up the computer can probably do it. Even cleaning up the background is possible if you have the right programme (I use Adobe) and skill.

I also use the digital camera to take pictures of the model and to enlarge the results and examine for imperfections in finish,

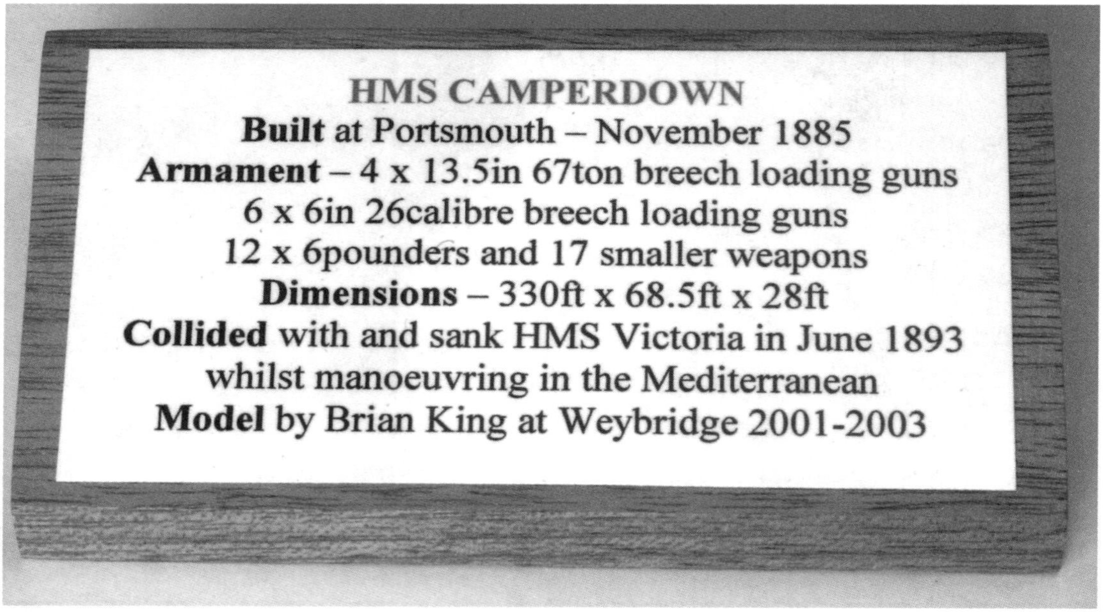

**HMS CAMPERDOWN**
**Built** at Portsmouth – November 1885
**Armament** – 4 x 13.5in 67ton breech loading guns
6 x 6in 26calibre breech loading guns
12 x 6pounders and 17 smaller weapons
**Dimensions** – 330ft x 68.5ft x 28ft
**Collided** with and sank HMS Victoria in June 1893
whilst manoeuvring in the Mediterranean
**Model** by Brian King at Weybridge 2001-2003

**Fig 3. Description plate for the glass case displaying HMS Camperdown.**

paintwork, etc,

The computer can be used to produce transparencies with details and they can be used for glazing e.g. Kent Clearview Screen detail on bridge windows.

The accuracy of the computer can be used in other ways e.g. dividing up lengths and angles, positioning components, etc. For example, when the shape of the formers for my 32ft gig were being plotted the edge of each former had to be divided up equally by the number of planks. The method of making the formers was to print onto sticky-back paper the shape and the divisions and these were used to cut out the plywood formers. With clinker built vessels the equal spacing marks are necessary, as the planks must be laid to these divisions. **Fig.2** shows the shape and divisions at stations 1 and 5.

Most computers also have a simple arithmetical calculator as well as a scientific type with sine, tan, cos and square roots, etc. This is useful when developing objects drawn in 3D into 2D flat shapes for your etching drawings. Alternatively you can use CAD for moving to and from 2D/3D and some programmes have a lofting kit, which is very useful when planking or plating hulls.

The traditional legend plate on models has been an engraved brass plate usually lacquered to prevent tarnishing. It may be traditional but they are usually very difficult to read unless you get the light right. They are also very expensive unless you have an engraving machine. The fonts held in the computer enable you to select a suitable typeface for your legend. You can then experiment with the layout and colours before printing and mounting on a suitable wood block. **Fig.3.** If you so desire, they can be laminated for protection.

The computer can also be used for research either using the Internet or an encyclopaedia programme. Materials, plans, kits, etc can also be viewed and ordered on line. It is also a means of communication between you and other modellers as, for example, Model Boats Forum where you can chuck in your halfpennyworth where appropriate and even find the answer to all your problems!

## CHAPTER 33

**Above: The complex turret shape on Bouvet - computer derived. Below: The barbette shape on HMS Camperdown was calculated and drawn on computer and printed out and stuck onto the model as a guide for planking**

# 34. Computers and Modelling

## Part 2

Being the age I am my technical drawing skills were honed on a drawing board with scales, set squares, compasses, protractors and the like. The accuracy I achieved was nowhere near what can be achieved on the computer using a CAD (Computer Aided Drawing) programme. I had to draw my artwork for etchings twice full size to ensure that the final image was accurate enough, As the etcher reduced my drawings to size the errors were, of course, halved. However well I tried I could never imitate the computers denseness of colour and crispness of line. Therein lays perhaps, its greatest advantage.

As far as I am concerned, the computer is most useful in the preparation of the artwork required for photo etching.

Once a component to be etched has been designed and drawn using CAD it can be rubber-stamped any number of times. The accuracy enables thicker components to be built up from laminates easily. A typical example of this technique is the production of warship flag lockers. These comprise a shallow cupboard, say 6ft square, divided up into smaller boxes which can be produced by horizontal and vertical strips with half-width

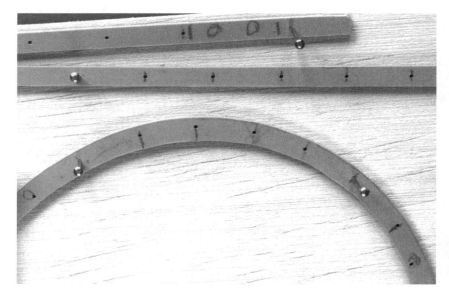

**Fig 1. Deck edging strips drilled for rails.**

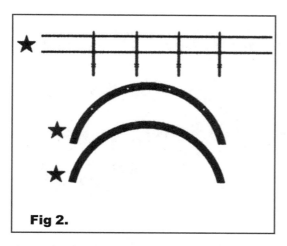

**Fig 2.**

symmetrical component and then mirror it vertically followed by mirroring the whole thing horizontally to produce the whole shape. Components such as door hinges and guard-rail stanchions can be grafted on from previous drawn detail, having been scaled in the process. This saves time and produces continuity of style in the work.

The Victorian battleship models I build usually have a narrow raised strip running around the deck edge. The guardrails fit into this (usually plastic) strip. The guardrails themselves are etched from 0.008in brass sheet. The design of this entails accommodating deck edge fittings such as bollards and fairleads as well as angular support struts here and there to counter the pull of the chains or cables between the stanchions. Guardrails can be quite complicated in fact.

Previously I used to drill the first hole for the end of the guardrail sequence, house the first stanchion in this and then proceed to drill subsequent mating holes to suit the stanchion spacing on the etching. This sounds simple but sooner or later you miscalculate where the

slots joined together like an old-fashioned egg box. Etching these strips is easy but joining them together usually ends up as a nightmare. I have found a better way is to produce a grid and laminate a number of these grids together to produce the depth. In case you have not fallen in the little boxes are used for signal flag stowage.

The computer can easily change the "hand" of drawings (mirroring). This can be used in many ways: one is to draw say a quarter of a

**Fig 3. Curved inside surface of the jig for drilling mast ladder rung fixing holes**

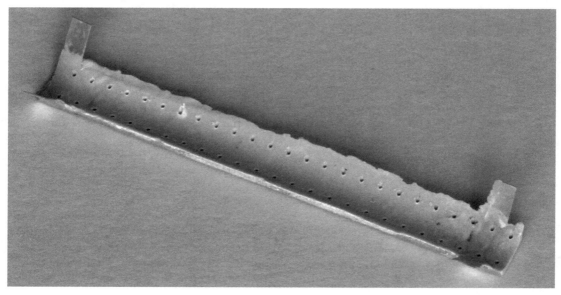

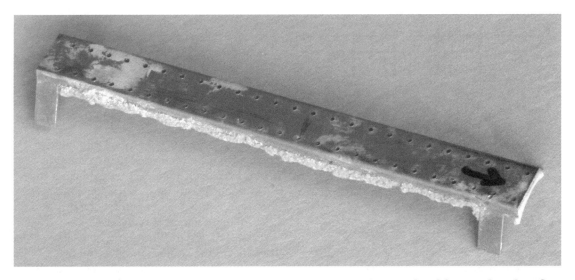

**Fig 4. Mast drilling jig outer surface - this shows the etched brass basis of the jig. Guide holes are drilled from this side.**

hole should be. This results in trying to stretch the etching into the hole. This is disastrous to the "lay" of the etching. This can only be overcome by trying to drill another hole so close to the original that it all goes pear-shaped or making a large hole and filling it in. Neither of these solutions is good.

It occurred to me that a better way of fitting the guardrails would be to drill the holes in the edging strip first allowing for the aforesaid bollards, fairleads, etc but before nailing these edge strips down they could be scanned and the pitch of each pair of stanchions measured and used to space out the guardrail etching drawing itself. **Fig.1** shows the drilled deck edging strips. With curved strips you have to measure the length around the curve and not the chordal figure of course. Just think how the metal strip will lay. If all this is done carefully the strip can be easily slotted into place with the minimum of handling. The first method always involves a lot of handling and consequent possible distortion of the strip. With easier assembly longer strips can be contemplated. Joins in guardrails are not good news, neither are joined capping rails if fitted. The capping rails can be etched: one copy with

holes matching those in the edging strip to locate the top of the stanchions and a second copy without holes to sit on top. **Fig.2** shows, top – the guardrail designed to accommodate a capping strip; note the short locating pins above the top rail at each stanchion point. The two curved strips shown below are the capping strips; the upper one has holes to suit the stanchions (if you can see them on the reproduction). The lower curved member is the blank capping strip, which sits on top. The stars are merely to show the forward end of each component.

Guardrails can be joined either by butting and gluing or soldering (difficult) or by half-etching the two end stanchions and fitting them in the same hole. If done carefully you can't see the join.

Although not the first thing you think about the etched work can contain drilling templates. An example would be a drilling template for accurately drilling the double column of vertical holes for those hull, funnel, etc ladders that consist of just rungs fixed to a vertical surface. **Figs.3 and 4** show such a template (jig) complete with Isopon. The U-shaped brass template with four arms embraced the

## CHAPTER 34

**Above: Guard rails are etched and located with the aid of the computer.**

lower mast of my model of HMS Camperdown. Because the rungs were set wide just using this jig in this state would not have worked, as the drill would have tried to slip round the circumference of the wood mast. To avoid this the mast was wrapped in clingfilm and the "trough" of the jig filled with Isopon. The two were then mated giving a curved, close-fitting inside face to the jig.

The holes were then drilled into the Isopon through the jig. When used to drill the mast the point of the drill was supported right onto the wood and could not "wander". **Fig.3** shows the mating curved surface of the jig and **Fig.4** the outer face. Laying out such templates is far easier and more accurate than trying to mark out and drill from first principles.

# 35. Life Saving Gear

Nearly all ship models will have some life-saving gear that will have to be made and, as it is usually in a prominent position, requires care otherwise it will let the rest of the model down.

## Lifebelts

Some of these will exist somewhere on most models. My problem used to be what are their dimensions? Easy if you have one to hand to measure. When I visited HMS Belfast I measured one which, for the record, was as follows: 30in external diameter, 24in internal diameter and 5in thick (their cross-section, at least modern ones, is more of an ellipse than a circle). Of course modern types are plastic, which has replaced the old painted canvas on cork type. I heard a story about an incident at

**Fig 1 & 2. The grills protecting both lifebelts illustrated below are products of photo etching.**

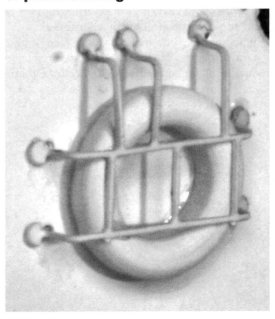 

**Fig 3. Life belt stowage on HMS Magnificent.**

one of our most important testing tanks where someone fell in. A wall-mounted life belt was snatched from the wall and thrown in whereupon it promptly sank! The cork had disintegrated leaving only the painted canvas shell! **Fig.1** shows a life belt protected by an etched grill on the hull and **Fig.2** shows a protective grill over a stern-mounted life belt both on HMS Camperdown. **Fig.3** shows the life belt stowage on HMS Magnificent.

## Breeches Buoy

A life belt fitted with short canvas breeches to provide support for the person using the life belt.

## Carley Floats

These are found on naval vessels. They have now been replaced by much improved life rafts that provide a fair degree of weather protection, which Carley floats certainly did not. Basically as far as the modeller is

**Fig 4. British style Carley float.**

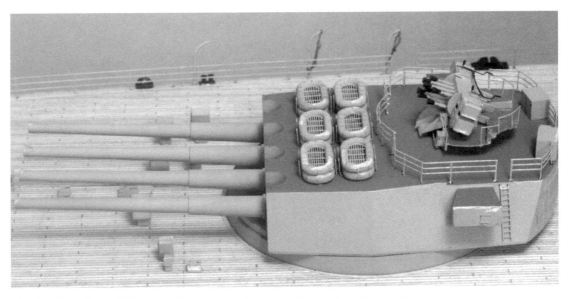

**Fig 5. Stacks of Carley floats on the "X" turret of HMS Anson.**

concerned they consisted of an external float made from copper tube with a grating of wood and net hanging down inside so you sit on the tube with your feet supported by the grating. The tubes have life lines on the outside to hang on if you are in the oggin. Whether in the raft or hanging on outside you got wet, cold and probably died from exposure

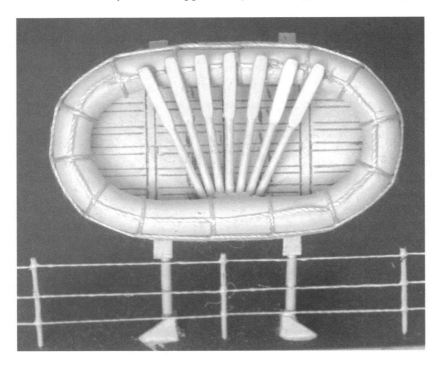

**Fig 6. Typical Carley float paddle stowage.**

**Fig 7. Cased inflatable stowed on an Arun life boat.**

quite rapidly. British Carley Floats are usually rectangular with semi-circular ends but American ones are often rectangular with rounded corners. **Fig.4** shows the British version. They were often stacked on the deck or hung from the superstructure. **Fig.5** shows the stacks of Carley floats on X turret of HMS Anson.
According to the size required they made from bent up wire or rod. Unless you are very skilled avoid using tube as it will kink given the slightest opportunity. Make sure you get what should be straight, straight. Nothing looks worse than curved sides. People will get the idea that you don't know your job!
I make a Perspex master and use this to make a two-part silicon rubber mould and then cast them in polyurethane resin. If you are clever they can be cast in David's P38 Isopon. Just fill each half of the mould and then press together. Make sure when you make the mould you provide locating bumps to ensure

positive location of the two mould halves. The gratings I etch but otherwise they will need to be made up from strips of wood. I also etch the paddles but squashed copper wire (squashed to form the blade) can be very successful. On such vessels as pre-WW2 aircraft carriers with rows of Carley floats along the deck edge, the paddles were often displayed in a fan shape, which looked very elegant. **Fig.6** shows this arrangement on my model of HMS Michael.

## Modern Inflatables

These have largely replaced the earlier emergency equipment. They are after stowed in a two-part cylindrical shell with hemispherical ends. **Fig.7** shows a cased inflatable and a Breeches buoy on an Arun lifeboat. When released they separate thus releasing the inflatable, which then proceeds to automatically inflate. The cruiser HMS

**Fig 8. Inflatable stowage on HMS Belfast.**

**Below: Collection of life belts ready to be suspended on aft of Bouvet.**

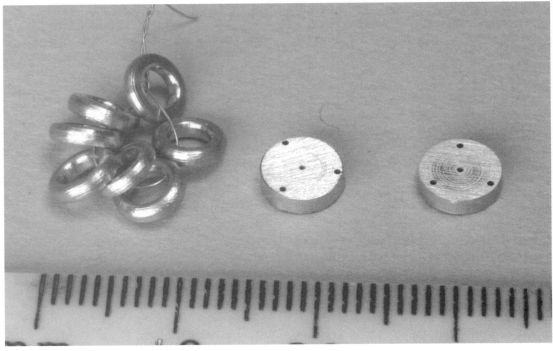

Belfast at present moored near Tower Bridge has rows of this type situated below the bridge and all are covered with canvas. Presumably they can be released by hand but a hydrostatic valve is also fitted that would automatically release them if the ship sank. The modeller is only faced in this case with making the stand and canvas cover.

Mine were made using the rectangular stand base as the basis, soldering on the four legs and the central hydrostatic valve gear and casting the canvas top in, I think, Isopon. To ensure release I always bury a piece of wire deep in the moulding before it sets. This enables it to be yanked out of the mould cavity - **Fig.8**.

# 36. Portholes

As in all workshop situations you inevitably come across odd problems. These may be ones you have had before and possibly never solved or indeed new challenges.

One such is drilling portholes in wooden hulls. This was a problem that came up in the Model Boats Forum some time ago but I was too busy at the time to add my half-penn'th. It is a problem I've had before and it has come up again with my model of Bouvet (1890's French battleship). I avoided the problem with HMS Camperdown by making the hull and superstructure sides as 0.008in brass etchings.

First define your problem. This is to drill a clean edged hole of the correct diameter and in the correct position on a curved wooden hull. On the face of it - no problem. The trouble with wood is that it has grain and objects to drills, which tend to tear the aforesaid grain and leave ragged edges to the hole.

That is the problem. Possible solutions are as follows:

Use a blunt drill. This goes beyond standard practice as normally this is a no no. A blunt drill turning very fast will blast, rather than cut, a clean hole. The problem is keeping up the speed and keeping the drill in position as it may tend to wander and also to produce a hole somewhat oversize. It may also throw up an edge around the hole but this is easily sheared of with a sharp scalpel or chisel. With some woods this works fine.

Drill a hole smaller than you need and enlarge it by grinding it to final size. This works well but you need a supply of small, low tapered grinding burrs. You need a few as the stone tends to disintegrate after some wear.

Use a multi-edged cutter. Looking closely at the basic problem you really need more than the two cutting edges provided by a normal twist drill. The best way to machine wood is to have many cutting edges moving very fast

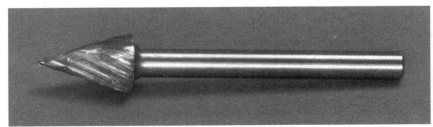

**Fig 1. Multi-edged cutter gives a clean cut in wood when used at high RPM.**

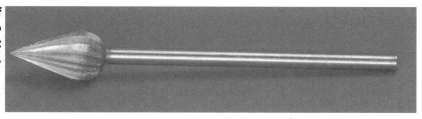

**Fig 2. A cutter of this shape will do as well as that shown in Fig 1.**

giving small chips but many of them. This prevents the tearing action of the twist drill's two cutting edges. With this basic appraisal I decided to examine my tool kit. Where it came from I have no idea but I found the cutter shown in **Fig.1**. It has multi cutting edges arranged in a spiral fashion and has a maximum diameter of 6mm. This cuts a very clean conical hole with an included angle of 35degrees. Using this first to cut the face of the hole to final diameter a normal drill can then follow on to complete the hole. This works very well indeed. Care needs to be exercised in marking out the position of the holes and again in picking up this position. Check before the full hole diameter is achieved whilst there is some chance of correction. Isn't life hard?

Use a teardrop burr. As shown in **Fig.2**, this should do the same job.

Use a slot drill. This may seem rather way out. However, because slot drills have flat cutting edges and have no centring point both work and drill need to be rigidly held in relationship which is usually not possible unless the component is small enough to be held in a vice or similar device. **Fig.3** shows a porthole fixture designed and built by Roger Antrobus. The miniature drill is held in two clips fixed to a moving slide. The angle of the slide can be adjusted to accommodate the slope of the hull. The transparent prism is a two-way spirit level as Roger always sets his models up plumb. Good workshop practice that!

## Glazing

Having got your hole you will need to glaze it. If are lucky and the size of the hole is the same as standard Perspex stock rod it is merely a question of putting said stock in the lathe and parting off. If the holes are not standard size you will need to turn it down before parting off. This is all fiddly, tedious stuff but it has to be done.

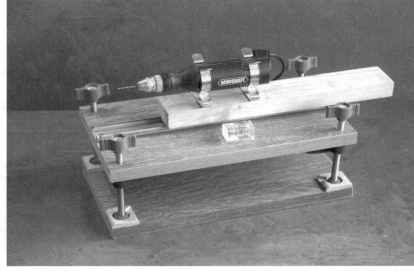

**Fig 3. A neat fixture for holding a modellers electric tool for porthole drilling.**

**Fig 4. Setting punch.**

Firstly keep all operations close to the chuck for maximum support. Only try and turn down enough stock to produce two slugs. It is tempting to produce as long a length as possible but attempting to part off any distance from the chuck jaws will result in the piece just shearing off. Make sure your parting tool is as narrow as possible (less than 1mm) and set it to exact centre height to avoid, as far as possible, a large pip. A narrow parting tool reduces the pressure on the work and saves material.

The last thing is to provide a receptacle for catching the slugs as they are parted off. I usually clean down the lathe, a rare event as my "friends" will tell you, to avoid loosing any slugs in the swarf.

I have in the past painted the pip end of the slugs with dark grey paint before insertion into their holes. To do this I stick them down onto double-sided tape and slap paint on the exposed ends. Whether this is necessary or not you must decide. Inserting them can be fun and you will need to work out a system for yourself. I normally put a dab of glue into the hole with a pointed stick, avoiding at all costs, getting any glue onto the surface. You can then hold the slugs with dividers but I find they twist and the slug catapults to the corners of the workshop never to be seen again. I now stick my slugs to a piece of sticky tape, insert them, and move the tape sideways, which releases the slug.

Sometimes the configuration of the parts

**Fig 5. Early experimental rigol fitting.**

## CHAPTER 36

**Fig 6. Unglazed portholes and rigols on Bouvet.**

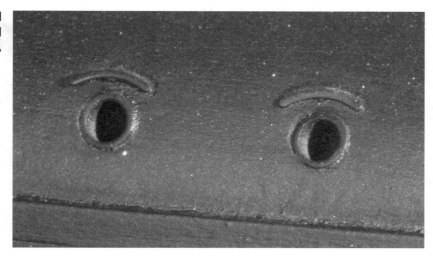

requires a brass frame around the slug in which case short lengths of brass tube need to be parted off, de-burred and inserted. **Fig.4** shows the setting punch used to insert the brass tubes. Incidentally if you find a slug has gone in too far it is usually better to punch it in further and add another slug. Trying to remove it usually does a lot of damage. If a tube insert goes in too far it can usually be retrieved with a bit of bent wire and a bit of strong language.

## Rigols or Eyebrows

For years I have been ignoring these hoping they would go away but they don't. Probably the simplest way is to bend them from wire and fix with varnish or paint. Sounds a bit impractical but it works so they tell me. To ensure the rigol is more secure I tried etching the rigol with two little tags sited at the top of said rigol and then they were bent together. I made a jig to position a drilled hole correctly above the port into which the tags were punched with the addition of some adhesive. **Fig.5** shows my original experiments with drilling portholes and rigol fitting.

If the side of the model is a brass etching as with my model of HMS Camperdown the rigol can be etched IN. This completely deceives the eye, which expects to see the rigol as a projection, not a depression as it really is.

**Fig.6** shows some of the unglazed portholes and rigols on my model of Bouvet.

# 37. Photographing your Models

One of the problems facing any columnist is what to write about next. One is always afraid of running out of subject matter. Somehow things turn up – if you are lucky.

I was sitting in my workshop working out guardrail spacing on a bridge piece from my present model of the French battleship Bouvet. The job was being illuminated by low winter sun shining **across** the piece, which showed up the imperfections. It looked like the surface of the moon! Hitherto the surface had been illuminated by light coming over my shoulder or at least at right angles to the surface and in that case the surface had looked more or less perfect. This illustrates the importance of lighting in assessing surface finish. The same effect is observed when flying. I learnt to fly at Fairoaks and we often flew over the Hog's Back, which is a long spine of land between Guildford and Farnham, which from ground level looks impressive but from the air almost disappears. Instead of carrying on with the guardrail spacing I spent the rest of the day cleaning up what I had thought was an immaculate piece of work! This sort of experience keeps you in your place.

You do see published, unfortunately, some pretty awful photos of models - out of focus, camera shake, etc. This is a dreadful shame as taking reasonable pictures suitable for publication should not be beyond someone who can build a fair model.

I thought a column devoted to the subject might be a good idea, so these notes are how I go about it. Not claiming expert status and not delving too deeply into the subject, as there are numerous books available on the subject anyway.

Firstly a basic understanding of the way your camera works is a good place to start. The three most important objects in your camera are the lens, shutter and aperture (stop) and how the latter two work together is most important. Whether the camera is digital (uses pixels) or analogue (uses film) the object of the lens system is to focus a SHARP image onto its sensitive surface. The shutter and aperture together allow the correct amount of light to give the correct exposure of the image. This can be achieved in a number of ways e.g. 1/50sec at f8 or 1/5sec at f22. To emphasize, both these combinations will give the same amount of light. So what? - you may ask – does it matter? The secret lies in the f-number or stop as this controls the depth of field. Different f-numbers have different depths of field, that is the band of sharpness

**Fig 1. Understading how to control depth of field can be used to make the desired image 'step out'.**

available for any given distance setting. For a sharp picture that area of sharpness must lie across the object being photographed. **Fig.1** shows a fully rigged seaboat where the f-number and focusing were designed to make the boat stand out from its surroundings, which are blurred. **Fig.2** shows an end shot taken with a large f-number rendering the whole length of the ship sharp with just the extreme stern beginning to show a fall off which does not matter at all.

If you are photographing a ship end to end as it were you will need a very large depth of field to ensure the whole length of the model is in focus. This will require you to stop right down to say f22 or even beyond if your camera will allow it. Remember the higher the f number the smaller the aperture (the hole through which the light passes) and in turn this will require a long exposure time, probably several seconds in which case the camera must be tripod mounted. In fact all such tabletop stuff needs a tripod and a remote (cable)

shutter release. To get a sharp image allow the camera to settle down after touching it, as it will vibrate even on a tripod. Keep perfectly still, especially if on a wooden floor. This applies to anyone else in the room as well and touch nothing whilst the shutter is open. You can use the self-timer on the camera to release the shutter instead of or with the remote. This should ensure the camera is absolutely still when it actually fires.

I remember trying to photograph in a press shop when I was in industry and although the presses were fixed to a concrete floor I could not get satisfactory results until the presses were stopped.

It is a good tip to remember that about one third of the depth of field lies in front of the focused point and two thirds beyond, so when setting up aim to focus about one third into the object. Some cameras allow you to stop down to examine what is in focus but I have never found this facility of any use.

It should also be understood that the depth

**Fig 2. Use a large f-number to keep the whole length of a ship model in focus.**

of field varies with the f-number of the lens. For instance a wide-angle lens of say f28 would have a much larger depth of field than a lens of f100. However, the latter lens would produce less distortion. Photographing the whole model usually requires a wide-angle lens to get all the length of the model in the picture.

With film cameras you can buy films of various speeds. For example taking pictures in poor light conditions or freezing fast movement you need a fast film ISO400 or above. The problem with fast film, however is that the grain size is large, which produces a poorer quality picture. With higher-grade digital cameras the sensitivity which is analogous to film speed can be altered. You can set it to ISO800 without loss of quality and this figure is probably conservative. This is a great advantage over film cameras. With cheaper cameras this may not be possible but this should not inconvenience you taking the sort of pictures we are talking about.

## Lighting

Having got the mechanics of the operation sorted you need to light the scene. I always use artificial light if I can as this is controllable whereas natural light can vary. Unless I am photographing workshop shots i.e. with the model under construction, I use my front bedroom which faces north and on a bright day I get nicely diffused, reflected light from the white painted houses opposite. However, I only use this as background lighting. The "business" is supplied by two flash units: Canon Speedlite 420EX and these are controlled by a Canon Speedlite Transmitter ST-E2 which sits on top of the camera which is an EOS 300D (digital).

One Speedlite points to the ceiling, which is white and gives a general overall diffused light. The other flash unit provides bounced flash onto a 12in circular white cloth reflector, which I direct onto the object being photographed. Using a digital camera you can quickly take a series of shots with this last light directed from several directions to see which is best. The exposure and contrast can be altered in the computer, as can be the cropping. I always leave a generous margin to allow for this. With the information in digital format all sorts of work can be done in the computer but I strive to avoid touching up, etc if possible as it takes time.

You will also need coloured sheets to act as backing for the subject to be photographed. Art shops have racks of coloured sheets. They vary in thickness from thick paper to light card. Select a few sheets of various colours and always store them away from the light

otherwise they will fade. Do not photograph things against a busy background. This is particularly likely if you photograph in the workshop rather than pose your shots. Remember we have talked about using depth of field to keep everything in focus but depth of field can also be used to put the background, or some other object, out of focus to make the subject stand out. However, this technique can look "arty" and should be used sparingly.

Finally not all pictures can be taken using a tripod and some will inevitably be hand-held. Up to now we have been discussing pictures using aperture priority. With hand-held stuff, to avoid camera shake, it is best to use shutter priority. Normally my technique is to select $1:250^{sec}$ as that should kill any degree of shake. If the resulting f-number gives me sufficient depth of field I go ahead. If it does not then I try more time until I get the depth of field that will do the job. The more light you have on the job the better but remember with advanced digital cameras you can alter the sensitivity analogous to using a faster film. There are now image stabilising lenses, which enable longer hand-held shots but of course these are expensive. If you want to take pictures of models to make them look real, on the water for instance, you must take them more or less at water level. Make sure any background is suitable.

Having got your digital pictures these must be transmitted to your editor. Be aware the larger the format and the greater the DPI (dots per inch) the better the final quality. It is up to your editor to tell you what he wants. However, I have to tell you some editors do not know what they want. In one case a publisher wanted all pictures submitted in A4 size seemingly without realising how big a computer file that represents. This information can be sent as an attachment to an email but remember that compression will degrade the image. You can also send it on a CD or DVD. If the photos are on film they will be scanned to produce a digital image.

# 38. Fittings
## Part 2

There is a tendency to consider when the hull and main superstructure are complete the model is, more or less, finished. The truth is that you probably will need more time for fitting out than you have already spent. You can cheat of course, by visiting your local model shop and buying what you need if you can find it but real scratch builders don't do that - do they? The trouble with bought out items is that they are rarely exactly what you want: slightly too big or small or of incorrect design and more to the point you didn't make them. The pain is how much time you need to research details and actually make them.

**Fig 1. Fore deck of HMS Camperdown. The hawse hole rims were resin cast.**

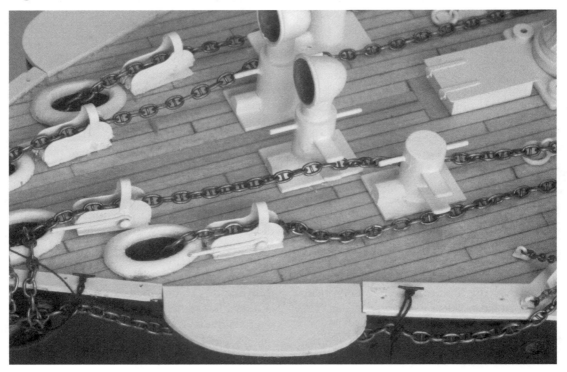

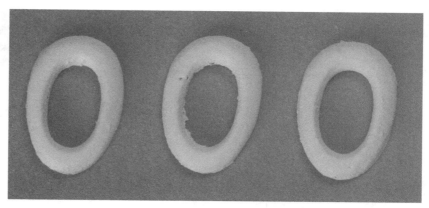

**Fig 2. Hawse hole surround resin castings.**

**Fig.1** shows the fore deck of HMS Camperdown. The rims (**Fig.2**) on the hawse holes were made in a silicon rubber mould (**Fig.3**) using Isopon and wiping it into the mould. The cowl vents were originally pressed out of annealed copper sheet but this requires a large gas blow-torch. Making them in ABS or styrene sheet using the same tools (a shaped male former and a female die consisting of a radiused round hole as shown in **Fig.4**) is simpler and quicker **Fig.5**. Most fittings were placed on a sheet of plastic,

which served as a base. The chain stoppers were etched and folded, as was the hatch cover. This latter was etched with the hinges attached and these were simply folded over on assembly. This meant their position was pre-determined and you only had one piece to worry about rather than three if the hinges had been made separately. In this case the body of the hatch was a Perspex block. The bitts were turnings. The little cleats around the margin were made by tightly folding a piece of wire leaving about 8mm folded and then

**Fig 3. The silicon rubber mould used to cast the hawse holes in Fig 2. above.**

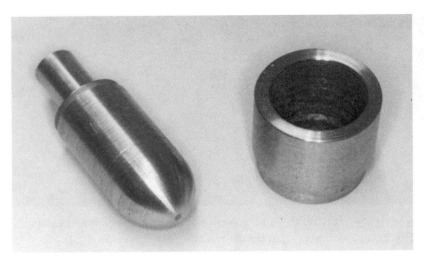

**Fig 4. Cowl vent forming tool designed to shape annealed copper but also works with ABS or styrene.**

splaying the arms out. If they are then soldered this will hide how they are made. You simply paint and bury the folded bit into the margin. These cleats were to provide supports for the looped anchor chain of the port anchor. The chain was obtained from JoTika Ltd the only people I know that can supply studded chain which was always used for anchors as it does not kink and is stronger than normal chain.

**Fig.6** shows a capstan which was a straightforward turning job but make sure you get all the subtle changes in diameter right. The whelps (the vertical ridges parallel to the axis) on the drum of the capstan prevent rope slippage. They were made from sticky back paper printed grey to match, in this case, the capstan dome. The shape was drawn on the computer. This method is much easier than cutting from metal sheet, bending to suit the curvature of the drum and then attempting to solder on. You get into the game of soldering one on and two drop off and you have to clean up afterwards, which is difficult to do properly.

The eyebolts shown in **Fig.6** consisted of an etched rectangular plate with two holes. The ring used the old technique of winding a

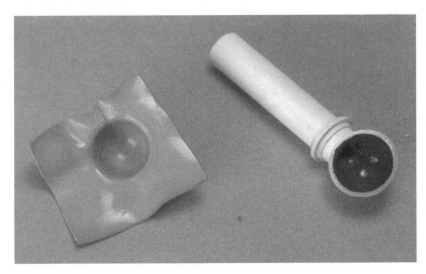

**Fig 5. The unfinished plastic moulding shown alongside a finished ventilator.**

**Fig 6. Capstan and eyebolts.**

**Fig 7. Fairleads can be fixed with an extended spigot machined onto the body.**

**Fig 8. Diffusers for fitting to the top of steam pipes.**

spring in brass wire and cutting the coils to form separate rings. Any helix remaining in the rings was taken out to bring the two ends together for soft soldering and cleaning up to produce a perfect ring. This was attached to the plate with an inverted loop of wire which was either soldered or glued into the plate, the two ends providing a fixing into a hole in the deck.

Bollards and Fairleads. These are always needed and not usually in only the one size. When making bollards I usually turn the cylindrical parts with a fixing spigot on their lower ends. These fit into a plastic or brass base plate and are fixed either by gluing or soldering. **Fig.7.** If the spigots are made long enough they can also be used for final fixing purposes. I drill oversize holes in the deck which I fill with glue or Isopon that allows last minute adjustment of position and does not require too accurate hole positioning (perfect for the lazy modeller). They can be moulded of course using a silicon rubber mould with the parting line vertical through the center line.

Fairleads are more difficult again usually required in more than one size. Their design varies slightly throughout the ship. For instance bow-mounted fairleads are often designed to take ropes at an angle rather than at right angles. Some also have rollers in their jaws. I usually hack mine out of Perspex sheet but when faced with many of the same design I have made moulds and castings. Cut a strip of Perspex the height of the fairlead; the thickness of the sheet being the width of the fairlead. Mark out the shape of the fairlead and drill four holes: two to define the opening and two to define the shape of the outside top of the jaws. The rest of the profile can then be cut/filed out. All working corners need to be well

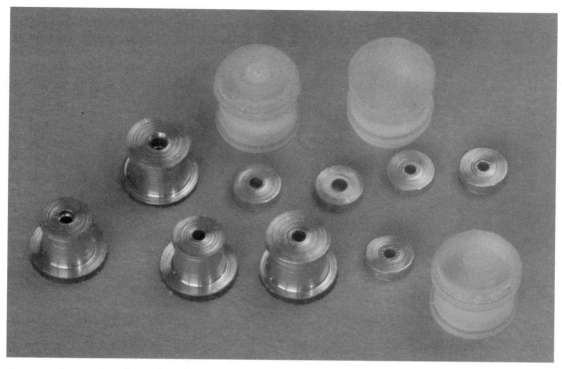

**Above:Searchlight parts ready for assembly and fitting to Bouvet.**

rounded and a slot cut into the top to accommodate the rope. All in all a nice little carving job. If the holes are carefully marked out and drilled, making a number of near identical fairleads is not to difficult - just a little boring perhaps. Alternatively you can make one master and from this a two-part mould in silicon rubber followed by casting in urethane, which may prove not to be so boring and require less skill but your castings will need to be cleaned up.

**Fig.8** shows some diffusers for fitting at the top of steam pipes. The developed length was calculated and the shape etched. Forming the etching into the cylindrical shape required was likely to be difficult as the thin rim at the end of the slots was likely to do all the bending thus leading to a multi-faceted shape and not producing the true cylinder required. It was a case of annealing and then hammering round a former until it got the idea. Really the essence of all forming operations; your will against what the material wants to do.

# 39. Making Plastic Castings

I have been asked to explain how plastic casting is done using either polyurethane or polyester. The advantage of castings is that they all turn out the same, or should do, and once a master pattern and mould has been made producing a number of identical parts should be relatively easy. Spend a lot of time on the master as the better that is obviously the better the castings.

## Silicon Rubber Moulds

Obtaining relatively small amounts of silicon rubber may not be easy. You only need enough for the job in hand as the shelf life is limited. Some model supply houses stock it but I use Hobby's of Knights Hill Square, SE27 0HH. The manufacturers will only supply quantities requiring a second mortgage.

You will need a leak-proof container large enough to house the object with enough space around it for adequate thickness of silicon rubber. I make a simple card box from a cereal packet sealed with Selotape.

You then fill the box with either Plasticene or PlayDoh to a depth, which will house half of the pattern. Make sure the Plasticene/PlayDoh is

worked up to the pattern to provide a positive, clean joint. The surface need not be absolutely flat, as you will also need to make some location dimples in the surface to locate the two halves of the mould – these are most important. The second half of the mould must locate accurately otherwise the finished casting will be "stepped". Paint the surface with Vaseline or diluted washing up liquid and allow to dry.

Mix up the silicon rubber according to the manufacturers instructions and stand to allow de-bubbling to take place. When this has occurred pour the solution into the box. Pour slowly down one side of the box and allow it to slowly envelope the pattern. This is to prevent the formation of air bubbles, which ruin the final casting.

When it is cured, invert the box, cut off the base and remove all the Plasticene/PlayDoh and re-treat the exposed mould face before pouring the second half of the mould. You may need to build up the sides of the box to get an adequate depth of silicon rubber before you pour. When that cures tear off the cardboard and separate the mould halves which you may find difficult.

You then need to decide where you are going

to pour into the mould and how you intend to get the trapped air out. If this air cannot escape malformed and incomplete castings will result. Cut these channels with a sharp scalpel. Every high point (with the mould in the pouring position) needs a tiny groove to allow the air to escape. Remember the deeper the pouring sprue the greater the hydrostatic pressure driving the plastic into the mould and the "sharper" the result.

You must decide where the parting line will come on the object. Silicon rubber being flexible will tolerate some undercuts whereas rigid material will not. You can obtain liquids to add to the mix to increase the flexibility of the silicon rubber but at the expense of some strength. The choice is yours but it really depends on the shape and complication of your casting together with the number of castings you need to take from the mould. Unfortunately some silicon rubbers will inhibit the surface curing of some polyester casting materials. Check with your supplier or run some tests for yourself. Urethane is not

**Fig 1. Ornamental carving on HMS Empress of India.**

inhibited but get a slow setting resin as some go off so fast they leave no time for mixing, de-bubbling, pouring and settling.

**Fig.1** shows the ornamental carving on the bow of HMS Empress of India and **Figs.2** and **3** show the pattern and moulds for same. This relic of sailing ship practice extended into the Victorian navy. HMS Victoria's carved bow work was quite extensive as

**Figs. 2 & 3. Pattern and moulds for HMS Empress of India bow carvings.**

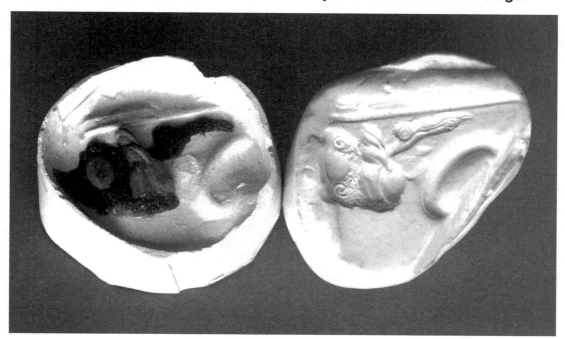

**Fig 4. HMS Victorias bow carving.**

shown in **Fig.4.** To simulate these carvings, Plaster of Paris casts were made of the bow area on which the actual carvings were made up in dental wax. Impressions were made and castings produced which were glued to the hulls. **Fig.5** is the dental wax master for Victoria's bow (note the metal studs representing balls round the shield) and the right hand is a moulding of this from which the appliquéd pieces were cast. The main feature was a shield carrying a coat of arms presumably Queen Victoria's. This was painted on – quite a job! The rest of the carving was painted with gold paint.

**Fig 5. Dental wax master for Victoria's bow.**

## CHAPTER 39

**Fig 6. The master for the mould for a turret on HMS King George V.**

**Fig 7. Below - the silicon rubber mould produced from the above.**

Fig 8. Below - single part mould for casting an anchor.

**Above: Turrets on completed HMS Queen Elizabeth.**

**Fig.6** shows the master for a between-decks turret for the low angle/high angle secondary armament of a King George V battleship. The silicon rubber mould produced from this master is shown in **Fig.7.** This mould is very flexible enabling easy removal of the component. Note the domes and dimples used to locate the two halves of the mould. The mould for (on the left) and the casemate (on the right) are shown in **Fig.8.** This mould

is only one part and much more rigid than the anchor mould, enabling Isopon or similar to be forced into it and smoothed off leaving a flat surface to apply to the hull. You must get the Isopon out of the mould whilst still in the "green" state as in this condition it is still somewhat flexible and it can easily be draped onto surfaces that are not perfectly flat. The thin roof over the gun port was added afterwards as it was too thin to cast.

# 40. Lines and Sections

The shape of a complicated thing like a ship's hull can be defined in two ways. A series of horizontal slices through the hull can be drawn; these are known as waterlines. Alternatively a series of vertical slices parallel to the keel can be used. These are known as buttock lines - **Fig.1**. I always use waterlines (drawn in colour on **Fig.1**) but at least one well-known kit maker tells me he prefers buttock lines. It matters not which you use -

the final result should be the same.

The ship's lines you are working to will probably give you both. Let us assume you decide to use waterlines. You may find that those given to you on the plan are not really what you want. Something on the hull such as an armoured belt or the thickness of the timber you have does not suit at least some of the waterlines you have. Can you redraw the waterlines yourself? Yes, if you have a set

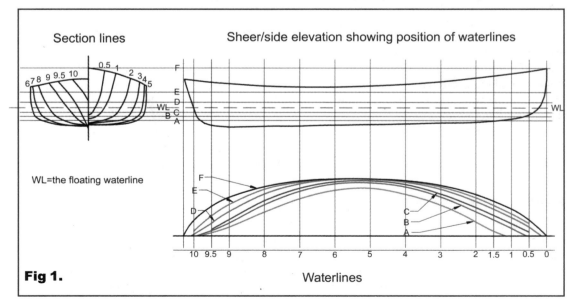

**Fig 1.**

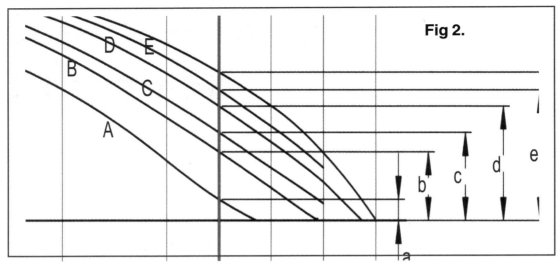

Fig 2.

of transverse sections.

If a horizontal line is drawn on the section at the height you want, the dimensions from the vertical centreline to the hull side at every station can be measured off and plotted on the plan. A free curve can then be drawn through these points and a new waterline created. The sheer (side elevation) will give you the intersecting points at the bow and stern and these can be projected down onto the plan. The critical areas in this work are the plan profiles at bow and stern particularly if the station lines are not close together. You really need a "half number" station position at these points. You can, of course, plot for yourself a half number on the section drawing making a shrewd guess at its shape from the two adjacent sections. Looking at the section lines as a whole will show you how the hull shape changes as it runs fore and aft from the mid section and should give you a fair idea of the shape of any new section plot.

## Plotting an extra section

To enable an extra template to be made to aid carving the hull at the bow and stern it may be necessary to plot extra station(s). **Fig.2** shows one such station marked X. Its position is between stations 1 and 2 where the

shape of the hull changes relatively quickly unlike amidships where there is little change in shape over quite a distance.

You will note in **Fig.2** the distances from the vertical centre line of the hull (the lower line) are measured and marked a, b, c, d, e, f. These dimensions are plotted on the sections drawing **Fig.3** and a line is drawn through them. This line must bear some relationship to the sections either side. Remember all three show, in effect, the run of the hull toward the bow.

## Plotting an extra waterline

You can, of course, use the waterline given on your lines plans. If you are using the lift system (bread and butter) your "lifts" must be the same thickness as the distance between the waterlines. Sometimes this is inconvenient: the available timber thickness is different or things like armoured belts or torpedo bulges call for a different spacing of waterlines. If you have the transverse sections these can be re-plotted. **Fig.4** shows the transverse sections with a new waterline marked Y. The intersection points at the station lines and their distances from the vertical centre line are shown in lower case - a, b, c, d, e, f. If these are now plotted onto the plan shown in **Fig.5** a new curve can be drawn giving you a new

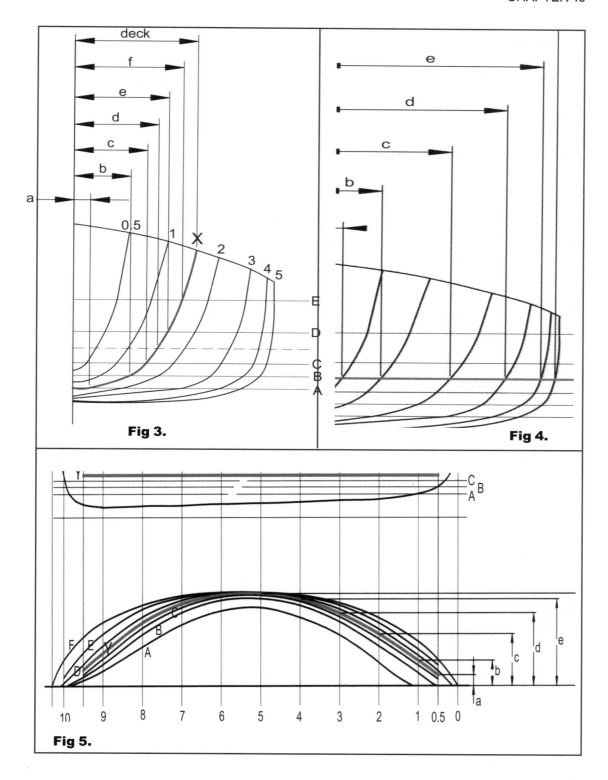

## CHAPTER 40

Fig 3.

Fig 4.

Fig 5.

| StationNo. | Waterlines | | | | | | |
|---|---|---|---|---|---|---|---|
| | DECK | E | D | C | B | A | W/L |
| Ht from datum | | varies | 23 | 8 | -7 | -13 | -19 |
| 0.5 | 23.5 | 18.5 | 13.5 | 6 | - | - | 9.7 |
| 1 | 40 | 33 | 27.5 | 18.5 | 11.5 | - | 23 |
| 2 | 61.5 | 57 | 51.5 | 42.5 | 36 | 21 | 47 |
| 3 | 75 | 73 | 69.5 | 62.5 | 58 | 46 | 66 |
| 4 | 82 | 81.5 | 80 | 76.5 | 72 | 62 | 78.5 |
| 5 | 84.5 | 84.5 | 84.5 | 82 | 79 | 71 | 83.5 |
| 6 | 84.5 | 84.5 | 84 | 80.5 | 77.5 | 68 | 82.5 |
| 7 | 81.5 | 80 | 77.5 | 71 | 66.5 | 55.5 | 74.5 |
| 8 | 73 | 69.5 | 62.5 | 52.5 | 46.5 | 35.5 | 57.5 |
| 9 | 57.5 | 47 | 36.5 | 24.5 | 19.5 | 13.5 | 30 |
| 9.5 | 44 | 30 | 19 | 10 | 7.5 | 5 | 14.5 |
| 10 | 23 | 7.5 | - | - | - | - | - |

waterline. This is shown marked Y and its position is also shown on the sheer (side elevation) above.

If you have understood the above you will be able to derive sections from waterlines and vice versa. In other words you will be a right clever clogs and master of all you survey shipwright wise!

Table of offsets for transverse sections and waterlines

Shipwrights use tables of offsets to define the shape of the hull. The horizontal waterlines are labelled A-E and their position relative to the "floating" waterline WL (the datum) is given in the horizontal column marked "Ht from datum". Note the dimensions above the WL are positive and those below are negative. The half-width of the vessel measured from the vertical centreline is shown for every station along the hull. Taking station 5 as an example the half-hull width is given as 84.5 at waterline E and 79 at waterline B.

The only other information you would require to plot sections and waterlines from the table would be the distance between the station lines and also the height of the deck at every station from a given datum probably the top waterline.

# 41. Idea Development

All model makers have problems and scratch building types have more than most. I make my ship's boats by moulding the shell using a male shaped mould in conjunction with a female mould usually consisting of only a profiled hole. The plastic may be polystyrene or ABS sheet although the latter, I find, requires more power to shape but probably has a longer life. Always keep plastics away from Ultra-Violet (UV) light sources as UV will degrade plastic. Some plastics are UV stabilised but I still protect as far as possible.

**Fig 1. First prototype assembly jig.**

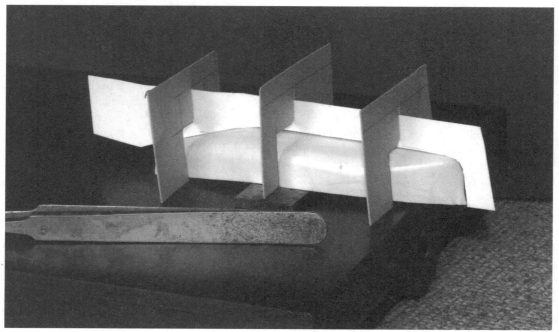

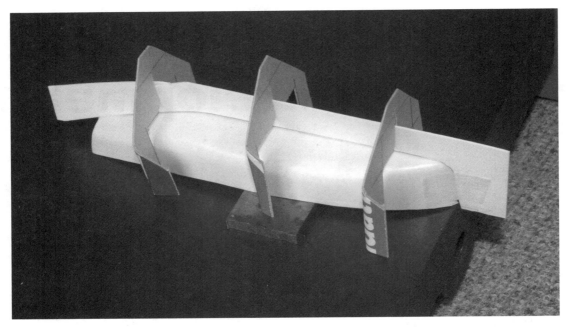

**Fig 2. Improved assembly jig - could be reproduced as a brass etching.**

The keel, rudderpost and stern post are cut as a wide rectangle from, say 0.002 in polystyrene sheet and this fits around the aforesaid moulding.

So far so good but the problem, on the face of it a very simple one, is how to secure the two parts together. In practice it is very easy to get the keel fixed to the shell but to get it stuck in the CORRECT position is very difficult.

This is a problem that has bugged me for years. I have tried using PlayDoh, BluTack, Plasticene, and strips of adhesive tape all with limited success together with bags of frustration and possibly even the use of the big D (apologies to G&S).

I finally decided to take my own advice and "lean" on this problem - give it some thought. The result of this entire "hard sums" problem was some cardboard jigs (fixtures really but jigs will do) which sit astride the upturned shell set up on my Engineer's Flat (surface plate). There is a slot cut for the keel which holds it vertical to the gunwales. You will note on **Fig.1** the shell is supported on a packing piece amidships to ensure this is so. To do the job properly you need several of these along the length of the keel. I made mine in fairly thin card to test the idea. The principle worked but as is usual with prototypes, improvements suggested themselves immediately. For one thing the cards tended to fall over (in a fore and aft direction). I cured this by folding the vertical edges at right angles to the body, one edge forward and one edge backward. This gave some stability but they also tended to be top-heavy so I snipped the top corners off as seen in **Fig.2**. The next time I do some etching I will make a whole series in brass. Being heavier they should work even better. Don't make the slot for the keel tight - it should be free enough to allow the keel to sit on the shell properly leaving no gap to fill afterwards. Ideally you need a jig close to the bow and one as close to the stern as possible for the maximum effect. The way to use these jigs is to set them up as explained and just TACK the two pieces together with the minimum amount of adhesive. I use thin

## CHAPTER 41

**Fig 3. Cardboard assembly jig - note the keel location slot.**

cyano for this. To avoid the cyano running along and attacking the jigs I snip off the lower corners of the keel slot. It can be a problem to stop very runny cyano from getting where its not wanted and steps to avoid this are very worthwhile. **Fig.3** shows a prototype card jig. Anyway if on examination the "tacking" is satisfactory apply cyano along the whole joint. If the keel is not in the correct position break the tacking, clean up and try again. You can break the tacking by physical means or by using de-bonder. However take care as some de-bonders will melt some plastics. A pre-trial is called for to make sure. Some manufacturers make a solvent free de-bonder, which largely avoids such problems. 5-Star Adhesives of Liverpool are one such but these de-bonders have a slower action than the normal type in my experience. Talking about de-bonders always make sure you have some close to hand and you know where it is. However careful you are sooner or later you will need some in a hurry.

I have gone through the above process of improvement which will be familiar to all those of you who have earned their living on a drawing board or in development. One started off with what in my day was called a "scheme". This was in effect a general assembly arrangement (GA) of all the parts fitted together - but this was only a start. This scheme was looked at by all and sundry particularly the boss and criticised from all angles. Will it work? Can it be simplified or made less costly? This in all probability resulted in another scheme with the process repeated several times until you get fed up with it. Finally the OK was given and you then had to draw out the details for the manufacturer of a prototype. If the job involved rotating or moving parts the limits and fit had to be worked out and eventually enough work had been done to enable the manufacturer to commence on a prototype. You hoped to heaven it would work and you hadn't made any serious mistakes.

I remember when working on machine tools we lads had a sneak look at the bosses work one lunch time only to find the elaborate scheme he had drawn, which looked fine on paper, could not be assembled in actuality. It is dead easy to draw things you can't make. Remember the 4 staircases in the form of a square all going up but they are still joined together. It ain't possible!

For the modeller always sketch out ideas you have and try and refine them on paper before putting the idea into practice. It's much more economical to do this than to make "n" number of actual prototypes at an appreciable cost in time and materials.

When faced with a problem enough thought will almost always produce an answer even if that answer is to do something else instead. Never loose hope. I remember machining a very difficult gun housing for my model of HMS Victoria. When drilling the last hole it picked up and smashed the Perspex component to the four corners of the workshop. No chance, in my workshop, of even finding all the bits. I was disgusted. After a little bit of thought I suddenly realised there was a simpler way of making it. I slept well that night!

# 42. Simulation

I was very interested in Colin Bishop's article "The Artful Bodger", in Model Boats because it really got to the bottom of many problems that worry scratch builders. Colin, being the sort of self-deprecating chap he is calls it

bodging but the essence of all model making is to make the model look like its prototype without necessarily making it the same way. In many cases that is clearly impossible to do anyway. Simulation is really the name of the

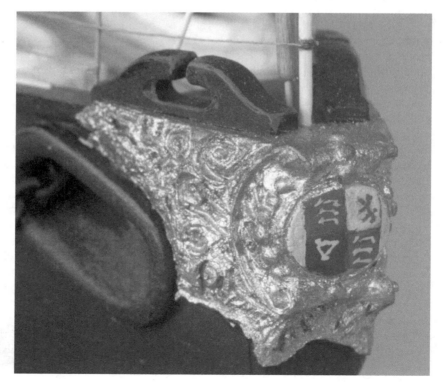

**Fig 1. Bow carving on HMS Victoria.**

**Fig 2.**

game. The skill of the model maker is to produce something that passes for the real thing but in truth may not be like it at all if looked at closely enough. Oil paintings are a typical example. Looked at very closely they look like a series of rather coarse daubs but looked at from the correct distance they look fine.

I remember building a model of HMS Victoria (1887) some 20 years ago. I had to paint Queen Victoria's coat of arms on a little shield about 8mm tall on the bow scrollwork. **Fig.1**. Ships were still carrying some bow decoration at that time although this was to disappear with the coming of the 20th century.

How to do this floored me for some time. It was then that I started to look at oil paintings and realised that a few well-chosen brush strokes of the correct colour in the right place were all that was necessary. The other necessity is confidence of a very high order -

a bit like cutting glass - any dithering and boy you are lost! After a bit of practice the deed was done much to my surprise. Faint heart never won fair lady.

Every problem requires its own solution, of course, although some general rules can be applied. For instance, faced with two thicknesses of wire, one too thin and the other too thick, always chose the thinner as you can always add a couple of coats of paint if necessary. Experienced model makers and particularly judges know by instinct if something is too thick. This is always a problem with injection moulded plastic kits – the technique prevents really fine sections being made.

The plastic industry also continues to over-emphasise detail to a phenomenal degree breaking yet another rule in the verisimilitude game. If you cannot get the detail fine enough LEAVE IT OFF. This also applies to GRP work. A number of guys have written to me

**Fig 3. Careful choice of grey shade for the anchors will make them stad out.**

saying that they had to spend a great deal of time cleaning off over-emphasised detail on bought hulls. They could have saved a lot of time by making the hull from scratch themselves. My answer is why didn't you? I think hull building is a great deal of fun and at least you then have total control over the degree of detail added and you have the added satisfaction of knowing the whole mess is yours!

Colour is another point. Always err onto the lighter rather than the darker and always try and add a bit of colour especially if it's a warship. Many years ago I built a working model of HMS Dreadnought (1906) from the plans prepared by my friend John Roberts. I painted it with Humbrol HN2 enamel, which at the time I thought was the correct Admiralty grey for the period. It looked dreadful; sombre was the word. I entered it into the ME where it was totally ignored by the judges. Since then I've learned

to get a bit of colour into any model. There are bits of colour on a warship if you look for them. Perhaps the Admiral's barge, if carried, is painted a different colour? **Fig.2**. What about the navigation light boxes, which used to be red and green but are now black of course. Various bits of forecastle gear are often identified as port and starboard with red and green.

Victorian era ships present their own problems. Their hulls are black with a confetti of protrusions all over them: hatches, outlets of one kind or another, ports, etc. With the light falling on them at right angles all this "busy-ness" disappears completely; all that work wasted. You need to do something about it to make at least some of it visible. For instance, the Victorian RN ships were using magnificent stocked anchors that could not be drawn up into the hawseholes so they had to be carried on anchor beds. If both the bed and the anchor are painted black the

**Fig 4. The boot topping on Victorian warships was very narrow - avoid the temptation to make it too wide.**

effect of the anchor and its stowing tackle is lost, so paint the anchor a dark grey of some sort to make it stand out. **Fig.3**.

The other essential feature of Victorian battleships is the narrow, very narrow, white boot topping. **Fig.4**. I've seen Victorian battleship models steaming away with great wide swathes of white boot topping and, for me, the essence of Victoriana is lost. Make this topping, on an average 1m long model, not more than 1/16in wide and lift the ends slightly to avoid giving the impression that the ship is "hogged" i.e. higher in the middle than the ends. I sweep up the first and last third about 2-3mm. This should not be obviously

apparent but leaves the correct impression - simulation!

Perhaps a word about degree of gloss. You used to see models it would appear coated with glass the gloss was so high. This has disappeared as it should, any ships even lifeboats and luxury yachts normally kept to a high finish, have lost their gloss if viewed at a model-sized distance. You cannot use a completely matt surface particularly on a working model, as it finger prints, so aim for a satin or eggshell finish. Lastly do not over-paint models as paint hides detail. This is unlikely if you spray as sprayed coats are only about 1/10th the thickness a brush coat.

# 43. Ladders

When building model ships it is not long before ladders are required. They vary enormously from simple rungs riveted or welded to some vertical surface; funnels, hull sides, etc to elaborate, highly decorated accommodation ladders, which form the official entrance to the ship. My model of the Italian battleship Duilio had one such with very elaborate Victorian decoration around the deck level platform. **Fig.1.** This could have been more elaborate if the ladder part itself had been in two parts with a central

**Fig 1. Elaborate decorative rails on ladder of Duilio.**

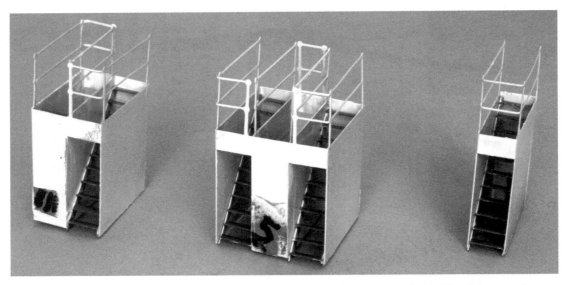

**Fig 2 & 3 Above and Below Left: Deck companionways fitted inside casings ready to fit into holes in the decks. Fig 4. Below Right: separate rungs attached to a hull side.**

"landing" to give ancient legs (like mine) a rest. Having made such a ladder it remains to fit it to the model, which usually requires some sort of structural work.

It should be remembered that such ladders could be carried triced up level with the deck when the ship is underway. When thus carried it may be impossible to pick them out on

photos taken about deck level although their shadow may give them away. There is always a davit above the sea end of the ladder and connected to it for hauling up or letting down. Three further details can add verisimilitude to a model. There should be a boat rope hanging down from the top platform for grabbing by the boat crew coming

**Fig 5. Mast rungs fitted into holes drilled using drilling template.**

**Fig 6. A different style of hull ladder.**

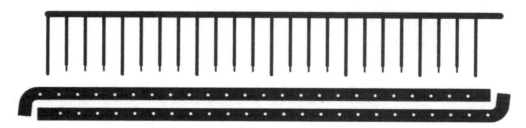

**Fig 7. Etched parts for round rung ladder.**

alongside. A fairly short mooring rope should be cheesed down on the lower platform and sometimes a wood rubbing strip is fitted where an alongside boat would rub. Such details can be garnered from Admiralty books of seamanship. These can often be found in second hand marine-type shops.

**Figs.2** and **3** show deck companionways. These have etched ladders fitted inside casings ready to be fitted into holes in the ship's deck. **Fig.2** shows a 2, 3 and 1 ladder arrangement whereas **Fig.3** is a 3-ladder set-up. The lower end of the ladders would need to be trimmed on assembly. The deck guardrails have been etched at the same time. Improvements could be added by fitting handrails to the ladders themselves. With this type I have also used milled or sawn Perspex or wood blocks for ladders as you cannot see through the steps and you can get away with it.

**Fig.4** shows separate rungs attached to a hull side. If you are etching, etch both the rungs and a drilling template; otherwise bend up the rungs from suitable wire. The strip of wood is to get the "stand-off" of the rungs equal and is left there to protect them. **Fig.5** shows

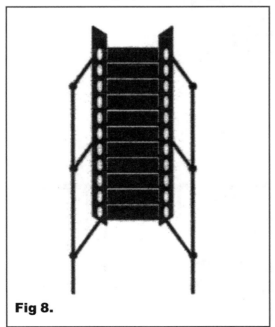

**Fig 8.**

similar rungs on a mast, which were also located using a modified drilling template that supported the drill onto the mast surface. Note also all sorts of juicy detail. **Fig.6** shows a different type of hull ladder. These are pieces of Perspex fitted into etched slots; the side of this model was an etched sheet of brass.

**Fig.7** is an independent round-rung ladder. I etch the rungs in the form of a "comb", slide the stiles on, solder and trim the excess off. The rungs aren't really round but at that scale who cares!

**Fig.8** is a drawing for an etched ladder complete with handrails and with oval lightening holes in the stiles – a detail easily put in when etching but so difficult to simulate any other way.

**Fig.9** shows an etched ladder blank without handrails. Fig.10 shows the first stage of bending to produce the ladder. It is important to fold along the whole length in one go to prevent stretching – **Fig.11. Fig.12** is the second stage of forming. This needs to be completed after removal from the folding bars. As can be seen the folding of the second stile is not quite complete; it should be at right angles of course. **Fig.13** shows the final folding of three steps. It is obvious that the success or otherwise of this operation depends on the "neck" of brass at each end of the step. When I prepared the etching drawings on the drawing board this could be a chancy thing. Sometimes the neck broke causing alarm and despondency all round. Now the computer is used for the drawing much more accuracy and consistency can be assured. In our book "Photo Etching" (No 36 in the Workshop Practice Series by Special Interest Model Books) Azien Watkin and I explain how this is done but space forbids repetition here.

I have never tried to make up a rope ladder at a small scale using full sized methods but etching can be used to simulate one. **Fig.14** shows one such. These are required if you rig a mooring boom to a model.

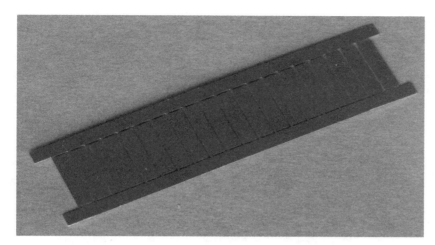

**Fig 9.**

**Fig 10.**

**Fig 11.**

**Fig 12.**

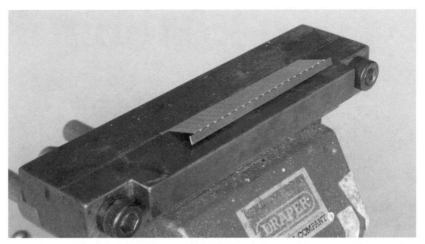

**Fig 13.**

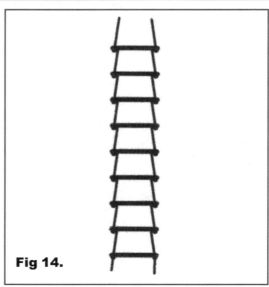

**Fig 14.**

# 44. Bending and Folding

All modelling sooner or later requires bending or folding skills. They may cause problems so I thought I would devote a column to them. Firstly a bit of theory. Practically all sheet, strip, rod, etc. is produced by rolling or drawing. They are what engineers call "wrought" materials as opposed to say cast or moulded. Rolled or drawn materials will have a grain, which will influence how they will react to bending. Wood too has a grain and this is usually obvious and most of us know instinctively that it will crack if subjected to attempts to bend it across the grain. Normally cast materials cannot be bent owing to their crystalline structure.

Other materials will not show any evidence of grain, at least by observation, but knowing in which direction it lays can be very important. The page this is printed on has the grain running from top to bottom and this is why it lies nicely and the pages turn well. You can check this by cutting a large square of material and holding it between your hands. Bring your hands together to make the sheet "cockle". You will find it "cockles" more easily one way than the other. The grain runs parallel to the edge you are holding. This, perhaps, works better with a square of cereal box or other light card. The grain normally runs parallel to the long edge of strip, bar or rod.

One other thing to bear in mind is that all this "working", as we greasy types call rolling, drawing, etc. is that it also hardens the metal. Metal may be supplied in this condition which may be so hard as to preclude any forming (folding and bending) without cracking. If it has been partially annealed it should be workable. In the fully soft condition it may be too soft for your purposes. An example of this - if you make ship's guardrails out of brass rod and then silver solder them together you find the brass rod has become annealed and lost its strength. Its former strength came from the drawing process that produced it. In that you have a problem: soft solder and the brass retains its strength but the joints are weak, Silver solder and you have strong joints and weak rods. You pays your money and you takes your choice.

When bending metal it is best bent across the grain (unlike wood) unless it's a VERY gentle curve when the opposite is the case. When I make funnels from either wood veneer or beer can aluminium the grain runs vertically. The material wraps around a former nicely that way! The secret here is not to glue the subsequent laminate to the former. It can

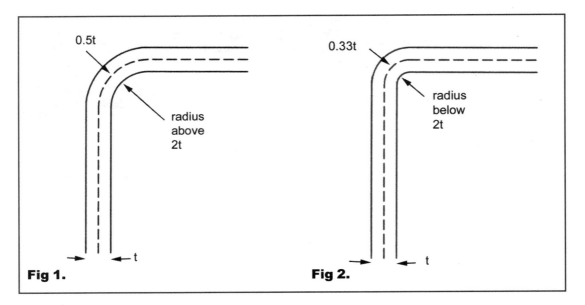

**Fig 1.**                    **Fig 2.**

quite spoil your day if you find the former cannot be removed. Fun it isn't.

If your vice jaws are in good condition these can be used for folding but it is probably best to use a set of folding bars as shown in my "Column" on Ladders. As I think I have mentioned the folding bars shown could have been improved by extending one end at least past the bolts which would have made them more universal in use. A pair of folding bars should be made up and kept just for folding; vice jaws by their very nature do tend to get knocked about. When folding items with a weak and strong feature it is best to clamp the more delicate end between the folding bars to protect fragile detail.

I know most of us want to do the job properly and to exercise the old brain matter I append the following. When bending a piece of metal into a curve the metal on the outside of the curve is stretched and that on the inside is compressed. Somewhere in between lies a point that is neither stretched or compressed but remains the same length. This is known as the neutral axis. It is the length of this axis that is the length of the blank required. For bends of radius greater than twice the thickness of metal this axis can be

assumed to be in the centre of the material. Tighter curves below 2t (where t is the thickness of the metal) need to compress the inside more but it is usually easier to stretch rather than compress material so for bending radii below twice metal thickness the neutral axis moves towards the inner edge and the figure becomes not 0.5t but 0.33t. See **Figs 1 & 2**.

**Fig.3** is a worked example in case I have not made it all crystal clear. What is the length of the neutral axis shown as a dotted central line? As the radius is above twice the thickness the radius of the neutral axis is: $7 + 1.5 = 8.5$
As the bend is a right angle we need 0.25 of the circumference of an 8.5R circle
Full circumference $= 2 \times Rp = 2 \times 8.5 \times p$
0.25 circumference $= (2 \times 8.4 \times p)/4 = 4.25p$
$= 13.35$ approx.
To this we need to add the two straight portions X and Y:
$X = 25 - (3 + 7) = 15$
$Y = 20 - (3 + 7) = 10$
Adding the curve $= 13.35 = 38.35$
Easy isn't it?
A moments reflection will show that the thicker the material compared with it's thickness the more extreme the stress will be

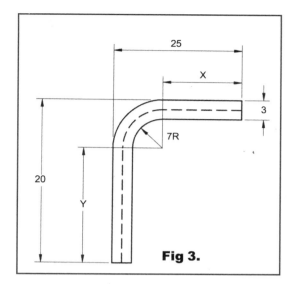

## CHAPTER 44

**Fig 3.**

blank before bending the amount used in the bend can be determined.

With long folds it is necessary to fold up the whole length of the fold together. If you "plough" fold the edge over you will stretch the outside edge and produce excess material which can be a right nuisance, as it will not lay flat.

If the fold is a 180° one you may, or may not, need to planish it flat according to how tight you require it. If you do need to planish make sure you cover the whole area before attempting to hammer flat to avoid marking the surface. **Fig.4** shows a hammer specially made for planishing. Note the head has a large, flat, polished face and a semi-spherical pein on the other end. Also notice the hammer handle is shaped to fit the palm of the hand. If you do acquire one use it only for planishing – do not hammer nails in with it or otherwise misuse it. For those unfamiliar with the word, planishing means to give a final finish by hammering or rolling to produce a smooth surface.

on the extreme fibres (inside and outside) and the more likelihood of fracture on the outside of the fold. This is why you can often fold thin, ductile material any which way and get away with it.

You may well need the above information if you are designing parts for etching.

Alternatively you can form the bend in a piece of scrap instead. If you scribe two parallel lines of a known distance apart on the scrap

**Fig 4. Small planishing hammer**

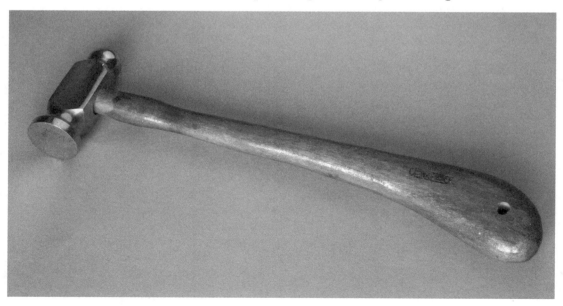